THE LEGACY & WISDOM OF
DR. MYLES MUNROE

YOU ARE A
KING

ACCESS THE UNLIMITED
RESOURCES OF GOD'S
ABUNDANT KINGDOM

DESTINY IMAGE BOOKS BY DR. MYLES MUNROE

Understanding Your Potential
Understanding Your Potential Expanded Edition
Unleash Your Purpose
Waiting and Dating
Wisdom from Myles Munroe
The Principle and Power of Kingdom Citizenship
Keys to Experiencing Heaven on Earth
The Legacy and Wisdom of Dr. Myles Munroe
You Are a King

DESTINY IMAGE® PUBLISHERS, INC.

P.O. Box 310, Shippensburg, PA 17257-0310

"Publishing cutting-edge prophetic resources to supernaturally empower the body of Christ"

This book and all other Destiny Image and Destiny Image Fiction books are available at Christian bookstores and distributors worldwide.

For more information on foreign distributors, call 717-532-3040.

Reach us on the Internet: www.destinyimage.com.

ISBN 13 TP: 978-0-7684-7665-1
ISBN 13 eBook: 978-0-7684-7666-8

For Worldwide Distribution, Printed in the U.S.A.
1 2 3 4 5 6 7 8 / 28 27 26 25 24

To Him who loved us and washed us from our sins in His own blood, and has made us kings and priests to His God and Father, to Him be glory and dominion forever and ever. Amen.

REVELATION 1:5-6 NKJV

CONTENTS

FOREWORD

For if because of one man's trespass (lapse, offense) death reigned through that one, much more surely will those who receive [God's] overflowing grace (unmerited favor) and the free gift of righteousness [putting them into right standing with Himself] reign as kings in life through the one Man Jesus Christ (the Messiah, the Anointed One) (Romans 5:17 AMPC).

THE APOSTLE PAUL INTRODUCES A POWERFUL DIMENSION OF living that many have not tapped into—that through right standing with God, in Christ, we would "reign as kings in life through the one Man Jesus Christ."

I will never forget Dr. Myles Munroe introducing the revelatory (and revolutionary) idea that you and I—the joint heirs of Christ Jesus—are indeed *kings*. This theology will undoubtedly provoke you; it certainly did me. But Scripture is filled with this language, and it demands our consideration. It will push you beyond "status quo religiosity," which continues to incorrectly remind us that we are something, or someone, we used to be.

We are "sinners saved by grace" (see Ephesians 2:5). We *were* sinners. Jesus saved us from the penalty of sin by grace—and that marvelous grace of God supernaturally translated sinners out of darkness and conferred a whole new status upon them, upon us. Totally unearned and deserved, but affirmed by Heaven nevertheless.

Jesus is identified as the King of kings. So, who are the *kings* over whom He is the sovereign King? You! Dr. Munroe brilliantly communicates what it means to be a Kingdom citizen in these powerful devotional entries. You are royalty. You are a son or daughter of God. You did absolutely nothing to achieve or attain this role except *believe*. Nevertheless, there is a world full of believers who are living beneath their status as kings.

This is not a title we use to exercise dominance over people, try to get our way, or even dare position ourselves in some arrogant, better-than-thou posture. It's time to simply be the people who rule and reign on earth, who subdue the spiritual forces of darkness that push back against God's good design, and function as Kingdom-of-Heaven representatives in the here and now.

The King of Glory lives within us. He took up residence within redeemed humanity to function as a Kingdom citizen—and for you to operate in that identity is to bring your thoughts, actions, and lifestyle into agreement with Jesus. This is what it means to function as a citizen of Heaven on earth—you are a king!

LARRY SPARKS
Publisher, Destiny Image
November 2023

INTRODUCTION

MOST PEOPLE BELIEVE THAT WE LIVE IN HUNDREDS OF DIF-
ferent countries, large and small, that cover the face of the
earth. We order our lives according to the governments and
cultures of those countries. We eat the food that the earth provides and we raise our families. It's all we've ever known and it's
all our parents and grandparents and great-grandparents ever
knew. We believe that we are stuck with what earth has to offer.
We limit our whole lives to what's on the planet because that's
the way everyone has been living for thousands of years.

However, we have lost touch with reality.

Even those of us who claim to know the ultimate King
(God) do not understand that we also belong to a country that
supersedes any of the known countries. We think of "the Kingdom of God" as a term pasted into prayers and sermons like an
add-on. We don't consider it our home country any more than
Mars. We think the Kingdom of God and Heaven comprise
some kind of invisible future destination above the clouds.

The truth about the Kingdom is difficult for people to
understand. I always feel as if I'm battling against 2,000 years

of mental block. We've been so conditioned to think "religion" that God has difficulty getting through to us the real message He delivered to us through Jesus Christ—which is about His Kingdom and how much He wants us to be full citizens of it, even while we're still living on this globe. In fact, He wants us to be royalty!

God's message is personal. Anyone who claims Christ as Savior becomes a citizen of the Kingdom of God, yet too many leave their citizenship on the shelf. They consider their faith to be religion, not citizenship, and they don't realize that it should be making a difference in every detail of their personal, earthly lives.

You can't see citizenship; you must experience it. In the same way, you can't see the Kingdom of God; you must experience it. This book, divided into 90 devotional-type sections, will help you experience the Kingdom of God and the Kingdom of Heaven, which are the same.

God, the King, has set up His Kingdom as earthly outposts, or colonies, populated with His citizens. The story of these colonies has not been an easy one. When Adam and Eve declared independence from Heaven, they had to set up their own government. God's Holy Spirit was no longer their "Governor," because they didn't want Him to be.

So Heaven started to seem like someplace far away. We lost the language, the culture, the values, the morals, the convictions, and the lifestyle that should have been the standard for any earthly colony of the Kingdom. We became aliens to God.

Because God wanted to turn that scenario around, He sent His Son Jesus to make sure we would know about the

Kingdom again. Once we find out how we fit into the Kingdom of God, everything is reversed. We begin to feel like aliens on planet Earth. We feel as if we belong someplace else. We also rediscover the present-day benefits that come with our heavenly citizenship, our royal place in the Kingdom.

It is my great passion to introduce people to the fullness of their citizenship in this heavenly Kingdom. You will see as you read that the Kingdom of God has almost nothing to do with religion. Instead, it has everything to do with the King Himself—with replicating His character and reproducing His will on earth. Maturing in their citizenship, Kingdom citizens grow to reflect their King's culture, values, morals, nature, and lifestyle.

"Kingdom" is not my idea—it's God's idea. I don't know why we ignore the obvious. Almost every book of the Bible has some reference to the Kingdom. Jesus talked about His Father's Kingdom all the time. But we do not. Instead, we talk about the Church and Christianity.

I have a serious problem with people who define the Kingdom of God too narrowly, in terms of one denomination or a single ethnic expression of faith in Christ. Yet I have an equally serious problem with people who define it in mushy terms, as if almost everyone living on earth is a Kingdom citizen without even thinking about it.

Like the people who are profiled in chapter 11 of Hebrews, we should be looking instinctively for the Kingdom of Heaven. We all miss Heaven, but most of us can't figure out what we're missing. We are missing our home country:

- We miss the lifestyle of peace, love, and joy.

- We miss the place where the streets are paved with gold and nobody has to steal it.

- We miss the place where the crystal-clear air is filled with joyful singing instead of smoke and gang violence.

- We miss our heavenly Father and our older Brother, not to mention all of our other brothers and sisters who belong to the King.

- We miss all of that, and somehow we think we must wait many years before we can go there. Not so.

The Kingdom of God is a present-tense place. It is an exciting place to call home. Let's explore together this Kingdom where we sit as royalty with Him!

And You have made them a kingdom (royal race) and priests to our God, and they shall reign [as kings] over the earth! (Revelation 5:10 AMPC)

1

IN PURSUIT OF POWER

For the Kingdom of God is not just a lot of talk; it is living by God's power (1 Corinthians 4:20 NLT).

THE PURSUIT OF POWER IS ONE OF THE MOST SIGNIFICANT motivations of the human heart. The passionate desire to manage our circumstances and environment seems to be built into the entire human race.

To the best of their ability, people work hard to control and improve their surroundings. Within any culture, people learn the "rules of the road" so that they can either follow them—or break them. Even acts of rebellion or aggression, whether isolated to a single individual or initiated by an organized army of soldiers, can trace their origin to this desire to control and dominate.

Young children cry and squabble to get the things they need and want. When a boy climbs his first tree, he is seeking to conquer new territory. When a girl picks a bouquet of flowers, she is trying to create something beautiful. As children mature, they gain knowledge about the world around them, and they put that know-how to use, striving not only to survive but to thrive.

This innate urge to manage the prevailing circumstances causes people to band together to accomplish things. Starting with family units, people organize themselves into towns, cities, geographical regions, and nations. They identify themselves as residents and citizens of the places where they live and work. Together, they share resources, face challenges, and train their children to do the same.

Live in God's power as royalty in His Kingdom.

2

KINGS AND TERRITORIES

Your kingdom is an everlasting kingdom,
and Your dominion endures throughout all
generations (Psalm 145:13 NKJV).

ANYTHING CALLED A KINGDOM IS A PLACE WHERE SOMEONE
called a king has dominion over something. No king can have
dominion unless he can claim ownership over territory. For
centuries, kings vied for territory all over Europe. They could
call themselves kings or lords because they owned vast acreages
of land, and whatever was in the land became their property—
their kingdom. Every field of barley, road, and river, every fox
and tree and rat belonged to them.

Whenever one king grew strong enough to invade another
king's property, he could extend his holdings. The greatness of
his kingdom was measured by the amount of land he possessed.
Kings formed armies of soldiers to protect their territory and
to invade neighboring regions. The armies were funded by the
resources of the king, and in the same way the farmers who

worked the land depended on the king's largesse, even as they turned over most of their crops and livestock to the king.

Nothing in the experience of modern governments equips us to understand this concept. The president of the United States does not own the whole country. The prime minister of England does not own the country he governs, and neither does the king of England. But in a true kingdom, everything becomes part of the king's personal property, every mountain, all of the roads, the animals and plants, the food and the water. No king can claim rulership unless he possesses territory, which makes all kings products of their property.

God's all-encompassing Kingdom territory is gained "'not by might nor by power, but by my Spirit,' says the Lord Almighty" (Zechariah 4:6 NIV).

3

A Kingdom's Glory

*Yours, Lord, is the greatness and the power
and the glory and the majesty and the splendor,
for everything in heaven and earth is yours.
Yours, Lord, is the kingdom; you are exalted as
head over all* (1 Chronicles 29:11 NIV).

THE GLORY OF A KINGDOM IS DETERMINED BY THE SIZE OF the king's territory. That is why kings love to expand their kingdoms. The history of kingdoms is a story of expansion. A king must have territory. He must have something to rule. He must be wealthy and strong and decisive. And he must desire to be the king. No part-time or reluctant kings need apply for the job.

The king embodies the essence of his kingdom. The kingdom issues forth from him. His relative permanence instills confidence. May I suggest that your president or prime minister does not embody your country? He is not permanent enough. In fact, he has only a part-time job.

A democracy or a republic is not the same as a kingdom. If you are looking for stability and consistency, don't put your faith in somebody who will be in charge for only four years or so. Your mortgage is twenty-five or thirty years. Wouldn't you like someone to be in charge at least longer than your mortgage?

The king is the center and the heart of a kingdom. People have to obey the sovereign king. There is no arguing with him or voting him out of office. We know what it is like to disagree with our elected officials. In fact, we tend to disagree quite loudly and even broadcast it on the news. But disagreement with a king puts you in peril for your life. You don't have to like what he says, but you have to obey if you expect to stick around.

A kingdom can be good, bad, or most of the time, a little of both. So why did the kingdom model turn out to be such a typical form of government?

The Lord is great and powerful—all glory, majesty, and splendor is His in His Kingdom in Heaven and earth!

4

THE FIRST COUNTRY

*It is I who made the earth and created mankind
on it. My own hands stretched out the heavens; I
marshaled their starry hosts* (Isaiah 45:12 NIV).

THE THINGS WE CAN SEE AND EXPERIENCE TURN OUT TO BE
the evidence of unseen governing influences, yet little do we
know what we are dealing with. We see both beauty and ugli-
ness, joy and suffering, harmony and conflict. "That's just life,"
we say. In reality, we have two worlds on one planet. Earth is
the name of the planet, and the two worlds that contend with
each other are actual kingdoms—the kingdom of darkness and
the Kingdom of light.

The kingdom of darkness has a ruler, and he stands in
opposition to the ruler of the Kingdom of light. Satan is one
of the names people have given to the prince of darkness. The
word *prince* means simply ruler, first, or fundamental ruler. On
the other side, people call the Son of God "the Light of the
world" or the ruler of the heavenly government.

Did you know that in Hebrew the word for *darkness* is the same as the word for *ignorance*? Similarly, the word for *knowledge* in Hebrew and Greek is the same as the word for *light*. So when we talk about the world or kingdom of darkness and the World of Light or Kingdom of God, we are talking about ignorance and knowledge.

We live in a world that is always tense with ongoing territorial conflicts of interest.

The way I see it is this: the Ruler of the Kingdom of Light created the physical place called Earth in order to extend the Kingdom of Heaven. He created it so that the people He was about to create would have something to rule over on His behalf.

I believe the earth was formed so that human beings could exercise co-rulership, so they could become regents for the King in Heaven. I also believe that Heaven is a real place, and that it is the first real country, the original one, and that all other kingdoms since the beginning of time have been mere shadows of the Kingdom (which I distinguish with an upper-case K because it belongs to God).

Believers are citizens of the Kingdom of Light—subject to God the King and co-heirs with the King's Son, Jesus.

5

HEAVENLY COLONIZATION

In this manner, therefore, pray: Our Father
in heaven, hallowed be Your name. Your
kingdom come. Your will be done on earth as it
is in heaven (Matthew 6:9-10 NKJV).

IN MANY WAYS, WE CAN SAY THAT GOD WAS SETTING UP A colony on earth, much as strong and wealthy countries have colonized parts of the earth. I know a lot about being part of a colony, because I am a native of the Bahamas, which was a colony of Great Britain until 1973. I was born under colonial rule. (I mention more about colonization later.)

But this "heavenly colonization" effort is still a work in progress. Most of what we see around us is the evidence of numerous conflicts between the colony of the Kingdom of Light and the kingdom of darkness.

When you serve under a king in a kingdom, you have the power to dominate your territory and to manage your assignment. What happens, however, if you lose your position? By nature, you are still a manager. Now you have been deprived of what you were managing. Now you have no purpose. When that happens—and it happens all the time—people latch on to whatever makes them feel comfortable and at least partially in charge of the challenges around them.

One of the major fallbacks is—you guessed it—religion. If you can't change your situation and you are trying hard to reconcile yourself to it, religion does a great job of helping. It makes you happy in your poverty, content in your illness, satisfied in your depression, and almost peaceful in your frustration. It works because it tells you that everything will be all right by and by. Your life will improve later. Religion tells you that Heaven is your destination, and all you have to do is hold out until you die. Religion postpones your reality to the future. It makes itself very attractive because it helps you accept things as they are when you feel you have lost control over your circumstances.

But...

*God's colony on earth is strong
and wealthy—and growing.*

6

RELIGION IS NOT THE KINGDOM

*What sorrow awaits you teachers of religious
law and you Pharisees. Hypocrites! For you shut
the door of the Kingdom of Heaven in people's
faces. You won't go in yourselves, and you don't
let others enter either* (Matthew 23:13 NLT
see also Matthew 23:15,23,25,27,29,34).

I AM MENTIONING RELIGION BECAUSE I DON'T WANT YOU TO
get off on the wrong track about the Kingdom. Religion is not
the same as the Kingdom I am talking about. It is a substitute. I
know that both "Kingdom of God" and "Kingdom of Heaven"
sound religious, but the Kingdom is something higher than
any religion in the world.

If the Kingdom of God is not the same as religion, what
is it? The original territory, or the first country, of the Kingdom of God is Heaven. So a kingdom is a government and the
Kingdom of God is God's government.

A king's decisions affect his territory and its citizens. A king is sovereign. He need not consult anyone else or get their votes. In other words, his will can become law. If he is a wicked, self-serving king, his expressed will can mean that the citizens will suffer. Just think what happened when people didn't obey the expressed will of ancient kings. One moment he could be lavishing a fortune on them and the next moment he could say, "Off with their heads!"

For better or for worse, then, a king's decisions and decrees produce the quality of life of his subjects. Over time, the king's declarations produce a culture for the citizens of the kingdom. It may be a culture of fear and poverty, or it may be a culture of freedom and peace.

God's Kingdom is a culture of
ultimate freedom and peace.

7

KINGDOM CHARACTERISTICS

Solomon ruled over all the kingdoms from the
Euphrates River in the north to the land of the
Philistines and the border of Egypt in the south.
The conquered peoples of those lands sent tribute
money to Solomon and continued to serve him
throughout his lifetime (1 Kings 4:21 NLT).

YOU HAVE MOST PROBABLY BEEN RAISED AND LIVE IN A COUN-
try considered a democracy or republic. Even in countries
with a king or queen, like England, the governing power and
authority does not reside solely in that one person. It can be
very difficult for most of us to wrap our minds around the concept of living as a citizen of a kingdom.

Our idea of the kingdom concept is insufficient, to say the
least. From our national culture as well as from our religious
culture, we sometimes get the notion that we can exercise our
vote for or against one of the King's laws or decisions. But it
doesn't work that way! Even when highly respected religious

leaders vote, for example, to promote a practicing homosexual into a position of high authority, they cannot change the moral standard of the King or His true Kingdom. The King of the original country (Heaven) is God, and He is the highest King of them all.

All kingdoms share specific characteristics, whether an earthly one or the heavenly one:

- All kingdoms have a king, who is born into kingship, not nominated and elected.
- All kingdoms have a lord, an owner. The lord and king are the same.
- The king's power is absolute in a true kingdom.
- All kingdoms have territory—the king must have a domain.
- The king personally owns everything in his domain.
- The king is never voted out of power in a kingdom.
- All kingdoms are a country, a nation, and are different from each other.
- All kingdoms have a constitution, a covenant the king makes with his citizens.
- All kingdoms consist of a group of people who identify themselves with a sovereign.
- All kingdoms have laws—strict principles by which the citizens must live.
- All kingdoms have citizens. Citizenship entails certain responsibilities and bestows specific rights and privileges.

- All kingdoms have royal privileges to which the citizens can have access through royal favor.
- All kingdoms have a principle of royal favor.
- All kingdoms have a code of ethics.
- All kingdoms have common wealth, which is why they are often called a "commonwealth"; the citizens have access to the same supply of wealth.
- Along the same lines, all kingdoms discourage private ownership.
- All kingdoms have a culture. This has to do with their lifestyle, clothing, values and morals, food, and even the way people respond to problems.
- All kingdoms have an economy and a taxation system.
- All kingdoms have a principle of giving to the king. Citizens never come before their king empty-handed.
- All kingdoms have an army. The soldiers are not civilians or ordinary citizens. (In the Kingdom of God, the army consists of angels.)
- The king's presence is the same as the king's authority. The king's name is the essence of his authority.
- All kingdoms have delegated authority.
- A king embodies the government of his kingdom. The government is not divided into branches or departments.
- All kingdoms have an educational system.

- All kingdoms have administration and organization.

- All kingdoms have a principle of glory, related to the sovereign king. The citizenry represents its king's glory.

- Similarly, all kingdoms have a principle of worship, directed toward the king but beneficial to the worshippers.

- All kingdoms have principles of reputation and provision. (This means that, for the sake of his reputation, the king must meet the needs of his citizens.)

- All kingdoms have a principle of decree. (Kings do not need to debate proposed laws, and their decrees cannot be changed.)

- Kings can choose their own citizens.

People are looking for qualities such as these. They would like a new economy. They would like to live under different laws. They want to experience royal favor and privileges. This is the kind of kingdom we seek. Even though all of us will remain subject to the restrictions of whatever country and municipality we belong to as long as we are alive on the planet Earth, we retain an instinctive passion for something bigger and better—the Kingdom of Light and goodness.

God's Kingdom is righteousness, peace, and joy.

8

GOD'S FAMILY BUSINESS

So now you Gentiles are no longer strangers
and foreigners. You are citizens along with
all of God's holy people. You are members of
God's family (Ephesians 2:19 NLT).

IF YOU DON'T UNDERSTAND THE BIG PICTURE OF WHAT GOD intended for the earth and its citizens, you can't understand your part of the whole story. What did God really want to accomplish when He created countless solar systems, millions of planets, and billions of stars? What was He thinking about when He made one of those solar systems with nine planets (or eight, if we can't count Pluto anymore)? What was His intent when He chose the third planet from that solar system's sun and put life on that planet? And what was He thinking about when He decided to put a piece of Himself into a "dirt suit" on that planet, creating something called man? What was He thinking about; what was He after?

Meantime, here on earth, what is the point of staying alive? Are we born just to make a living, reproduce by having a child or two, and eventually die?

Without knowing the big picture, most of us get involved in all of our rituals and we forget about our relationship with our Creator. We think that everything begins and ends with us. We are always scrambling to stay on top. Our lives never seem to have very much meaning.

If, however, you understand that the created universe stems from a parallel universe called Heaven, and that the Creator is the King who is always extending His territory, you can begin to recognize that you are part of a family business. In fact, being part of that family business gives you significance.

The Kingdom is a family business and our Father wants to extend His business into foreign territories. He wants His kids like you and me to run the Earth Department for Him.

*Your significance is found in being
part of God's family business.*

9

THE SEARCH FOR SIGNIFICANCE

*"For I know the plans I have for you," says the Lord.
"They are plans for good and not for disaster, to give
you a future and a hope"* (Jeremiah 29:11 NLT).

ALL HUMAN BEINGS ARE SEARCHING FOR SOME KIND OF SIG-
nificance, and their search manifests itself in many ways. All
religions attempt to answer the big-picture questions. All the
conflicts between religions come from the competing searches.
It is not just the Buddhists, the Hindus, the Muslims, the
Christians, and the other major or minor religions; even the
agnostics and the atheists are part of the same search.

The search is not bad, but as we know very well, the search
often becomes its own answer. We stop searching and make
the means the end. We get defensive about our own version of
the search and protective of our particular rituals. We set ourselves apart as members of our own particular group. We miss
the fact that there is more.

We are the King's kids. The King has been inviting us to realize that we are His children and to become full citizens of the biggest, richest, most glorious Kingdom we can imagine—and many have not heard His invitation. Instead, we have been fooling around like street urchins in some vacant lot, trying to change it into a playground.

The Kingdom is a family business and His intention was to have the Earth Department look a lot like the Headquarters. He wants to extend His experience from the invisible world to the visible world through His family members. He wants His Kingdom to come and His will to be done on earth as it is in Heaven.

Do you want to become part of the most important family business of all time?

COLONIAL RULE

Years passed, and the king of Egypt died. But the Israelites continued to groan under their burden of slavery. They cried out for help, and their cry rose up to God (Exodus 2:23 NLT).

I AM A CITIZEN OF THE COMMONWEALTH OF THE BAHAMAS. The Bahamas is an island nation in the Caribbean Sea that used to be a colony of Great Britain. All of the Caribbean island nations have colonization as part of their history—the Bahamas, Jamaica, Barbados, Saint Kitts and Nevis, Saint Thomas, Saint Lucia, Saint Vincent, Grenada, all the way down to Trinidad and Tobago, almost too many islands to count. Many of these islands are former colonies of Great Britain, and some of them are still British territories today.

The fact that I was born and grew up under colonial rule means that I am intimately acquainted with what it means to be a successful colony of another nation.

What is a colony? A colony is a territory under the direct control of a central, imperialistic government. The government, which was England in our case, considers the colony an outpost of the faraway central authority. Great Britain is on the other side of the Atlantic Ocean, 7,000 kilometers (4,300 miles) away, but those of us who lived in their territory of the Bahamas were considered English citizens.

Why do we use "the king's English" and not American English, even though the United States is much closer to our shores? Because of our status as a British colony for two hundred years. Generations of Bahamians were educated in that particular type of English, and all of our business is transacted in that language. Despite the fact that more than 90 percent of our population is of African descent, our ancestors having been brought to the islands as slaves to work on the plantations, very few of us know even a few words in our ancestors' native language, or their customs. I know next to nothing about African history. Instead, I learned in school about Sir Francis Drake and Sir Walter Raleigh and Oliver Cromwell. I learned the names of all of the long succession of English kings and queens. I read all of the plays of Shakespeare.

Great Britain gave Bahamians other distinctive features, as well. They gave us their long socks and short pants; they gave us neckties; they gave us a preference for straightened hair; they gave us knives and forks; they gave us their tea. The colonial influence is very obvious in the Bahamas.

"God heard their groaning…and knew it was time to act" (Exodus 2:24-25 NLT). *God remembers His own.*

11

SUPERNATURAL RESCUE

*So I have come down to rescue them from the hand of the
Egyptians and to bring them up out of that land into a
good and spacious land, a land flowing with milk and
honey—the home of the Canaanites, Hittites, Amorites,
Perizzites, Hivites and Jebusites* (Exodus 3:8 NIV).

IN TERMS OF THE KINGDOM OF GOD, YOU COULD SAY THAT
when you come into the Kingdom, you change colonies. But
it can take a long time to lose your old ways of thinking and
behaving just as in the Bahamas, where our culture to this day
is saturated with British ways despite years of independence
as a sovereign nation. When you come into God's Kingdom,
your personal life will carry many of your old ways as you learn
to think and behave differently to match your new affiliation.

Regardless of where we live on the globe, those of us who
are citizens of the Kingdom of Heaven were born as colonists of the kingdom of darkness. But somewhere along the
line we switched loyalties, joining forces with colonists of the

Kingdom of Light. When we switched, we began to shed our old habits and worldview, along with our old ways of thinking and our expectations. In time, we should begin not only to represent our new King, but to resemble Him.

When people become colonists in the Kingdom of God, they sign up for a steep learning curve, but it's worth it. You may or may not know what I'm talking about from personal experience. Unless we learn what it means to be a citizen of this earth-colony of the Kingdom of Heaven, we will miss all of the benefits that come with colonial status.

Colonization describes both a king's expansion of his kingdom territory as well as an expression of his personality. Colonization means that a kingdom has been extended to a distant territory, and after a time the colony can be expected to manifest the culture of the kingdom, even though the citizens possessed a different culture in their past.

Kingdom of God colonists encounter a steep learning curve, but the Holy Spirit is with each one every step of the way.

12

OCCUPY

He said, "A nobleman was called away to a distant empire to be crowned king and then return. Before he left, he called together ten of his servants and divided among them ten pounds of silver, saying, 'Invest this for me while I am gone'" (Luke 19:12-13 NLT).

Colonization does not always work out. Here is a 2,000-year-old parable about some of the difficulties of Kingdom colonization. It begins like this:

> *A certain nobleman went into a far country to receive for himself a kingdom, and to return. And he called his ten servants, and delivered them ten pounds, and said unto them, Occupy till I come* (Luke 19:12-13 KJV).

The "far country" is a new colony. The man went to that territory because he was supposed to receive kingship there. He left ten of his servants behind, giving them resources and telling them to transact business until he returned. "Occupy" is a word that implies not only staying behind to represent the owner, but actively conducting business. The nobleman wanted his servants to administrate and take control of the business in the place, and he told them that he would come back to check on them.

As you read the rest of the parable (Luke 19:11-27), an unhappy story unfolds that looks like the story of humankind on earth. The nobleman-king was rejected by the citizens of the new country.

Did the king appreciate this? Not at all. Isn't this just what we have done in many of our countries today? We have taken God out of our schools and universities, and out of our government. In the Bahamas we haven't decided to erect a legal separation of God and government, and I hope we don't ever do it, but in many other countries, that is the law.

The servants in the parable were instructed to "occupy" because their territory was never created to be governed without the king. But they did not. They took matters into their own hands, and the result was ruin. The stewards in the story blame their actions on their circumstances, and even on the master himself. *"I was afraid because you are a hard man to deal with, taking what isn't yours and harvesting crops you didn't plant"* (Luke 19:21 NLT). This sounds a lot like what King God finds when He checks on the people He left to occupy the planet for Him. We say this to God: "We think You are too harsh. We can't trust You. We prefer to do things our own way." Let this not be our response to Him.

The King is still bringing in the Kingdom, one colonist at a time.

13

LOOK AROUND

*But my people would not listen to me. They kept
doing whatever they wanted, following the stubborn
desires of their evil hearts. They went backward
instead of forward* (Jeremiah 7:24 NLT).

HOW HAS THE EARTH COLONY TURNED OUT? JUST LOOK AROUND
you. Does earth look like Heaven? Look at the bars on our win-
dows and the guns in our houses. Every day a murder. We are
afraid to jog outside, so we buy a treadmill. We are afraid to let
our children visit certain family members, lest they be abused.
We are unable to succeed in marriage, so the divorce business is
booming. We have got nothing to show the King except broken
lives, disease, depression, conflict, religious clashes, war, frustration, bankruptcy, tyrants and dictators, broken homes, and
broken nations.

Is it too late for us? I don't think so. The King is still bringing in the Kingdom, one colonist at a time. Yet the only way
we can occupy until He comes again is to change. We must

recognize that we can't do it on our own. We need the King to save us from ourselves. We need the Savior to save us, to salvage the colony. He is coming to bring in a new government—if we will accept it.

We should realize by now that none of the governments human beings have produced are working: democracy, democratic socialism, communism—none of them. That is because they all belong to the kingdom of darkness, ever since our earliest ancestors first declared independence from the original King.

Referring back to the Luke 19 parable, we need to realize that the King will be asking us to give Him an account. He will not care how your pastor did or how your boss did. He will want to know what *you* did with the resources He gave you to oversee.

He has questions for you. "I want to know what you have done to represent My Kingdom? How have you explained and expanded My Kingdom? Have you demonstrated integrity in your workplace? Have you been a good father or mother or child or friend? Have you made things better in your circle of influence? What is your attitude? Are you making investments with what I have given you? What kind of job are you doing?"

Do you have your answers ready when the King asks?

14

EARTHLING OR HEAVENLING

And I will give you the keys of the Kingdom of Heaven.
Whatever you forbid on earth will be forbidden in
heaven, and whatever you permit on earth will be
permitted in heaven (Matthew 16:19 NLT).

THOSE OF US KNOWN AS KINGDOM COLONISTS ARE NOT earthlings—we are "heavenlings" or "heavenians," if there can be such words. We are citizens of the Kingdom of Heaven. Many of us learned a prayer that includes these words: "Your kingdom come. Your will be done on earth as it is in heaven" (Matthew 6:10). When we pray this prayer, we are expecting the Father's will to be performed in our colony, just as it is in Heaven. We are acting out of our identity as true colonists who see themselves as full citizens of Heaven and representatives of the King.

Most organized groups within societies, including religions, function on the basis of membership. However, countries, nations, kingdoms—and their colonies—are different; they function on the basis of citizenship. This is an important distinction to make, otherwise you might assume that being part of a colony relegates you to some kind of second-class citizenship that is more like a club membership.

You need to know you are a full citizen of whatever nation claims your territory as a colony. This applies even to Heaven and earth. Heaven is the territory of King God, although it remains largely invisible to human eyes. Heaven is God's country. Heaven is an actual place. Sometimes people who have visited Heaven give us a glimpse of what it is like, and they report amazing experiences. Heaven is God's headquarters, where His throne is—not a fancy chair, rather the seat of power or citadel.

These two terms are used interchangeably: the Kingdom of God and the Kingdom of Heaven. They both mean the same thing, except the first one refers to the One who owns the Kingdom and the other refers to the territory.

You are a full citizen of the
Kingdom of God and Heaven.

15

GOD THE KING

You are my King and my God (Psalm 44:4 NIV).

THERE ARE VARIOUS DESCRIPTIVE TERMS FOR GOD. PEOPLE call Him the King of Glory, the King of Creation, the King of the Universe. He is the King of everything seen as well as everything unseen. He owns it all and He rules it from within His original territory, Heaven.

Often, those of us who dwell on the planet called Earth fail to understand the setup. We see the physical planet all around us, and we find it to be delightful and fearful at the same time. We may recognize the existence of a world outside of our immediate experience, but we do not understand its importance. We recognize our citizenship in some nation, but we don't realize that we all possess dual citizenship in a physical country or colony and in an unseen one—Heaven.

Those of us who are known as Kingdom colonists are not earthlings—we are "heavenlings."

Since the Kingdom of God is a country, a real place called Heaven, and since countries bestow citizenship on the people who dwell there, it is citizenship (not membership) that has been bestowed on the "heavenlings" who dwell on the colony called Earth. Citizenship comes with more guarantees and privileges than membership does, along with specific responsibilities.

You can become a member of a *community* within your colony or country, but your citizenship is what ties you to the community in the first place. In the same way, you can become a member of a religion or a branch of a religion, but your citizenship in the Kingdom of Light (or, sad to say, the kingdom of darkness) will take priority over your membership in that particular religion.

*As a Kingdom colonist, you are not
an earthling—you are a heavenling.*

16

FULL CITIZENSHIP

Consequently, you are no longer foreigners and strangers, but fellow citizens with God's people and also members of his household, built on the foundation of the apostles and prophets, with Christ Jesus himself as the chief cornerstone (Ephesians 2:19-20 NIV).

NATURALIZED CITIZENSHIP IS THE GOAL, NOT MERE MEMbership, whether you live in the primary country or one of its colonies. You need to pursue full citizenship in the Kingdom of Heaven as if your life depended upon it, because it does. As a citizen, you will grow to reflect the culture of the country, which in turn reflects the ruler of the country. Your life will be radically changed and improved as a result.

Citizenship is a legal position. Membership is more of an accommodation. You can apply for membership in the local lodge or Rotary Club and they can decide whether or not to accommodate and include you. They can also decide to de-member (I could have written dis-member) you, making you a non-member. But once you are a citizen, no one can take away your citizenship just because they don't like you, not even the government. (You can read how this applies to a citizen of the Kingdom of Heaven in John 10:28-29.)

Having legal citizenship entitles you to certain rights, and those rights do not depend on feelings or emotions; they depend on much more powerful things: position and law. You can switch religious affiliations or other memberships without losing your citizenship in the Kingdom, and people do. They get their feelings hurt or they offend somebody, so they move on. They change their minds about what they want to do, so they find a new place that will accommodate their viewpoint.

Pursue full citizenship in the Kingdom of Heaven as if your life depended upon it, because it does.

17

DECLARATION OF INDEPENDENCE

After sending them out, the Lord God stationed mighty cherubim to the east of the Garden of Eden. And he placed a flaming sword that flashed back and forth to guard the way to the tree of life (Genesis 3:24 NLT).

NOW EVEN THOUGH A COUNTRY WILL NOT REMOVE YOUR name from the citizenship rolls, a citizen can remove his own name if he or she chooses. In any kind of kingdom, that is called rebellion, and it happens all the time. When the American colonists wrote their Declaration of Independence, they were announcing their intention to renounce their English citizenship, to break off legal ties with that country, to establish their own independent nation.

Once you are a citizen, no one can take away your citizenship just because they don't like you, not even the government. Independence and private ownership are an abomination within a colony. They cannot coexist with a kingdom mentality.

To this day, the "American spirit" is the same as a spirit of independence, and a strong streak of individualism and private ownership has resulted in the growth of capitalism.

When the first man, Adam, declared independence from his government in the Garden, he resigned his citizenship by switching it to the kingdom of darkness. (Remember, darkness is synonymous with ignorance. Adam was ignorant of the importance of obedience to the single legal regulation of his government, and he was ignorant of the goals of his government.)

A declaration of independence results in the loss of citizenship. You may not even know what you are doing, but the end result is the same. If you change your mind, you may decide to seek citizenship again, and you may eventually be repatriated. But it will not be easy to regain your citizenship once you have lost it.

Value your citizenship in the
Kingdom of God above all else.

18

THE ORIGINAL COLONIST

Then the Lord God formed the man from the
dust of the ground. He breathed the breath of
life into the man's nostrils, and the man became
a living person (Genesis 2:7 NLT).

A NOTE HERE ABOUT WHAT THE HUMAN RACE LOST WHEN the first human being, Adam, declared his independence from his original King. We need to know what we are looking for if we ever hope to regain it. The human race did not lose residence in Heaven. The first human was created on earth and out of the earth. His residence was on earth. He never resided in Heaven and he did not fall from Heaven.

He was the original colonist, and he had been allotted full citizenship in the Kingdom of Heaven even as he dwelt on the earth. What he repudiated was his assignment, which was to exercise dominion over the earth in obedience to the King. When he refused to follow God's directions in fulfilling his assignment, that first man lost dominion and citizenship at the same time.

As the story goes, Adam's wife, Eve, was persuaded by a talking serpent, otherwise known as the devil, to eat some delicious-looking fruit from one of the trees in their garden paradise. Trouble was, that was the one and only thing their Creator-King, God, had instructed them not to do. They had only one rule and they broke it. So they got kicked out of their garden, and all of their children, grandchildren, and so forth were born outside of the colony territory—which means that none of them were born into citizenship in the Kingdom of Heaven.

Because of what the first man did, every one of the 8 billion people on earth and the 115,000 who were born yesterday are hungry for the Kingdom of God. It is not about going to Heaven someday—although most religions think so—it is about becoming repatriated into the Kingdom that our long-ago forefather lost. It is about resuming exercise of the dominion over the planet, expanding the original colony until it covers the entire globe.

The first man (Adam) lost dominion and citizenship in the Kingdom of Heaven— we suffer that consequence as well.

19

CONSEQUENCES

*And God said, "See, I have given you every herb
that yields seed which is on the face of all the earth,
and every tree whose fruit yields seed; to you it
shall be for food"* (Genesis 1:29 NKJV).

IN THE GARDEN, ADAM AND EVE HAD IT ALL—EVERY PROVISION and all the privileges that come with the assignment of stewardship and management. The Garden was the first settlement of the colony of Heaven, and the Fall changed all that.

We call this "the Fall" and yet we do not really think very much about what those first humans fell from. Innocence? Goodness? Obedience? Yes, but more importantly they fell from dominion. They fell down on the job by breaking the one rule or law they had been given. For two bites of fruit, they lost their citizenship in the colony of the Kingdom of Heaven. Through the Fall, earth was disconnected from Heaven. No longer did Adam defer to the direction of God.

It is about resuming exercise of the dominion over the planet, expanding the original colony until it covers the entire globe.

When you cut off the relationship with your kingdom, you have to set up your own government. Independence can be hard to live out. Ever since we declared our independence in the Bahamas, we no longer refer to England to make governmental decisions. We had to start running our own country. We encountered endless problems that we had never come across before, and we had to figure out what to do on our own.

Deferring to God's direction is always the best course of action.

20

HIGH TREASON

And the Lord God commanded the man, saying,
"Of every tree of the garden you may freely eat; but
of the tree of the knowledge of good and evil you
shall not eat, for in the day that you eat of it you
shall surely die" (Genesis 1:16-17 NKJV).

THE FIRST MAN'S DECISION TO DISREGARD GOD'S PROHIBItion and to eat of the fruit of the tree seems like such a minor thing. But God regarded it as high treason. Treason involves deceit and corruption. The highest form of trust had been broken. Adam not only disobeyed the one rule he had been given, he lied about it afterward.

If an ambassador of a country should sell the secrets of his country to another country, that is treason. In every country in the world, treason is punishable by death. That is why God, when He gave Adam the whole world to run, entrusted all of it to his stewardship, but gave him the one single prohibition and leveled with him about the potential punishment: *"You must not eat from the tree of the knowledge of good and evil, for when you eat from it you will certainly die"* (Genesis 2:17 NIV).

The pronouncement of the punishment of death revealed the gravity of the sin. The word *sin* means rebellion against authority. Now Adam and all individuals who followed him would find death inevitable. He had committed treason. The man himself could not undo the punishment. A new Adam would have to come from Heaven to do that, and He did. Jesus came to restore what Adam lost—everything.

*We can't undo the punishment
of death—but Jesus did, for us.*

21

GOOD OLD DAYS

As Pharaoh approached, the Israelites looked up,
and there were the Egyptians, marching after them.
They were terrified and cried out to the Lord. They
said to Moses, "Was it because there were no graves
in Egypt that you brought us to the desert to die?
What have you done to us by bringing us out of
Egypt? Didn't we say to you in Egypt, 'Leave us
alone; let us serve the Egyptians'? It would have
been better for us to serve the Egyptians than to
die in the desert!" (Exodus 14:10-12 NIV)

WHEN THE BAHAMAS WAS STILL A COLONY, THE QUEEN HARDLY
ever came here. In all my life, I think she visited twice. And yet
she was our ruler. This shows how a sovereign does not have to
come into the territory in order to claim it or retain it. What she
did was send a governor to live here. As long as he was here, the
queen was represented here. A succession of governors lived in

a big pink mansion known as the Government House on Duke Street in Nassau.

Naturally, when a colony declares independence from the home country, the appointed governor must leave. Here, this happened peacefully, but in other colonies it happens with violence. Then the newly independent government must set up its own structure and rules.

As the new country adjusts to its sovereign status, many citizens may long for the "good old days" when they were under colonial rule. Others will be perfectly happy forging an independent existence and creating a distinctive culture.

A new Adam would have to come from Heaven to do that, and He did. He came to restore what Adam lost—everything.

The only Kingdom government that will never fail is the one King God rules.

22

GOVERNORSHIP

Just as Death and Destruction are never satisfied, so human desire is never satisfied (Proverbs 27:20 NLT).

How does governorship translate into the Kingdom of Heaven and its expanding colony on earth? First of all, the native population cannot assume the colonial governorship role, although they can be loyal citizens. That role is reserved for a special, divine representative of the heavenly country known as the Holy Spirit. The earth-colony was never intended to function without its heavenly governor, but when humankind declared independence, He had to leave. The citizens lost their legal connection to their first country, Heaven. They threw off its constitution and rulership and culture.

As a result, we have inherited a mess. Our world today is a culture of death. We have become citizens of a country (the whole earth) that, minus the stabilizing influence of Heaven, has gone completely berserk. Fighting within our homes and waging wars overseas, we keep trying to control the out-of-control situation we find ourselves in, but we can't agree about how to do it. Can we get our first governor back?

Do you know the answer to our dilemma?

23

SOMETHING BETTER

For God had something better in mind
for us (Hebrews 11:40 NLT).

I HAVE VISITED MORE THAN SEVENTY COUNTRIES, AND MY passport really gets a workout. Sometimes, even though I have all the right documentation, I run into difficulties with the customs officials. I suppose they are just doing their jobs, but I think they sometimes overdo their jobs. The interrogations can seem endless. When that happens, I feel like telling my interrogator, "Look, I come from the Bahamas, and you are making me want to go back home. Do you realize what a wonderful place the Bahamas is? The average Bahamian citizen has everything. Everything is cool, man. No harassment." Times like that make me appreciate the benefits of my citizenship.

In the Bahamas, there are people from other Caribbean nations, such as Haiti, who are clamoring for citizenship. These people want to join themselves with our government or the government of nations like the United States; they are looking for some nearby jurisdiction that is better off than their own. Although Haiti is the oldest black republic in the world and the second-oldest republic in the Western hemisphere after the United States, it continues to struggle economically. Ordinary citizens face a multitude of problems. These are good people, but their governmental system continues to be ineffective.

As is the case in other countries with problems, you will find a very small group of people who are rich and a vast majority who are very poor. For the average Haitian citizen, the benefits of citizenship are limited indeed. They are willing to uproot their families and start over. By some estimates, as many as 40,000 Haitians are now living in the Bahamas, and a very large proportion of that number may be illegal immigrants. They know that legal citizenship status can be hard to get and that people must want it badly enough to work for it. They know that Bahamian citizenship would provide them with opportunities they cannot have any other way.

*Take time to really appreciate the
benefits of your heavenly citizenship.*

24

BENEFITS OF
CITIZENSHIP

*"No weapon forged against you will prevail,
and you will refute every tongue that accuses
you. This is the heritage of the servants of the
Lord, and this is their vindication from me,"
declares the Lord* (Isaiah 54:17 NIV).

By definition, a "citizen" is someone who owes allegiance to a government and who is therefore entitled to receive protection from mistreatment and also to enjoy special rights and privileges that come with citizenship. A citizen is automatically connected with the seat of power of his government. That is why people want to become citizens of successful and wealthy nations; once you are a citizen you can expect your life to improve. Why else would you want to go to all that trouble?

Citizenship is the most valuable asset of a nation. Because of its power, it is not easily given or obtained, and the current citizens of a nation do not readily want to share citizenship with outsiders. We are seeing this play out in many Western European countries at the present time because of the continuing influx of immigrants from Muslim countries. Such a large population shift has the potential to transform the entire religious, social, and cultural complexion of Europe. Weekly, we hear of sectarian riots and legal power struggles. The Muslim immigrants would not be moving into those countries if they did not offer the prospect of a higher standard of living.

The benefits of citizenship in a country with a kingdom system of government can far outweigh the benefits of citizenship in even wealthy nations that have non-kingdom forms of government.

From the United States, we hear reports of Mexican immigration challenges. In spite of checkpoints and an actual fence on the US-Mexican border, illegal immigrants pour into the southwestern states and move northward. Some legislators want to place all illegal aliens on a fast track to American citizenship. Others want to detain and deport them.

The benefits of being a citizen of God's Kingdom
far outweigh citizenship in any earthly country.

25

SEEKING CITIZENSHIP

Then the commander said, "I had to pay a lot of money for my citizenship." "But I was born a citizen," Paul replied (Acts 22:28 NIV).

CITIZENSHIP IS SUCH A VALUABLE STATUS THAT PEOPLE ARE willing to do wicked things to obtain it. They falsify documents or marry people they do not even know simply to get the advantages of citizenship. All immigrants, legal or otherwise, are seeking the privileges and benefits of the host country. They want jobs, higher pay, better health care, greater educational opportunities, and an overall better quality of life than they can obtain as citizens of their home countries. The best way to obtain improved benefits and rights is to become full citizens of a successful and well-to-do nation.

A citizen is part of an elite, privileged group, and people who were born into their citizenship do not appreciate their status as much as they could. Citizenship is easy to come by if you are born into it, but if you must seek naturalized citizenship you soon find out that it can be an arduous process. Citizenship status is too precious for governments to hand out indiscriminately like handbills.

You need to know that the benefits of citizenship in a country with a kingdom system of government can far outweigh the benefits of citizenship in even wealthy nations that have non-kingdom forms of government. This is because, ideally, the king's wealth will be distributed broadly to the citizens.

Only in God's Kingdom will wealth be distributed broadly and justly to the citizens.

26

♔

THE COMMONWEALTH PRINCIPLE

That at that time you were without Christ, being aliens from the commonwealth of Israel and strangers from the covenants of promise, having no hope and without God in the world (Ephesians 2:12 NKJV).

THE WORD *COMMONWEALTH* EXISTS ONLY IN KINGDOMS. When the Bahamas was part of the Commonwealth of Great Britain, the British built our roads and provided us with clean water. They brought us electricity and other upgraded services. They had their warships anchored in Nassau harbor so they could protect us poor little Bahamians.

A citizen of a kingdom who is in good standing with a king has more than enough of everything.

When we decided to declare our independence, all those types of assistance ceased. Independence means you have to manage your own affairs, pay your own bills, provide your own clean water, and maintain your own highway system. (Thus, our roads today are famous for being bumpy. We are no longer part of a commonwealth that pays for improvements.)

Because of the commonwealth principle, the citizenry in a kingdom begins to reflect their king's qualities, including his wealth. In extreme examples, you see something like the Palace of Versailles, which is so big that it would take three days to walk through all the rooms, with gold everywhere. It is the largest king's palace in the world. And that's just the house. King Louis XIV also had stables for his horses that were so extensive they would cover half of the Bahamas. Even today, those stables look better than the house I live in.

Three thousand people lived in the Palace of Versailles at any given time. They wanted to live there, of course, because everything was provided for them. Free housing. Free food. Free clothes. Free everything. Citizenship matters greatly. An individual's welfare depends on it.

Citizenship empowers and provides
access to a country's rights and privileges.

27

THE POWER OF CITIZENSHIP

This is what the Lord says to Cyrus, his anointed one,
whose right hand he will empower. Before him, mighty
kings will be paralyzed with fear. Their fortress gates
will be opened, never to shut again (Isaiah 45:1 NLT).

CITIZENSHIP EMPOWERS AN INDIVIDUAL; CITIZENSHIP PRO-
vides legitimate access to all the rights and privileges of a
constitution and a country. Becoming a citizen, especially a
citizen of a kingdom such as the Kingdom of God, means that
you become powerful. Your citizenship is the source of your
personal authority where those rights are concerned. You have
the power to demand things. By the power of your citizenship, you can call in constitutional privileges and promises. The
constitution is more powerful than the citizens, just as the law
is more powerful than the lawyer or the judge who exercises
it and certainly more powerful than the politicians who talk

about it. Good citizens have access to the full protection and advantage of the law.

Countries do not have members. You cannot be a member of the United States of America. You cannot be a member of Jamaica. You can certainly be a member of a religious group or an organization, but you would never say that you are a member of a country because membership does not entitle you to the full range of rights.

Citizenship is permanent, if you want it to be. Whether or not the people around you like you, you cannot be deprived of your constitutional rights by a consensus or somebody's whim. Once you are a citizen, you are no longer a mere member; you are a legal creature, which means the law protects you. You could even say that citizenship is dangerous. Law means you remove emotions and relationships from the equation. It doesn't matter who you like or do not like or who likes you. You are a citizen, regardless.

Citizenship in the Kingdom of God and Heaven
is the most powerful gift God can give you.

28

A COVENANT

*I set My rainbow in the cloud, and it shall
be for the sign of the covenant between Me
and the earth* (Genesis 9:13 NKJV).

YOU CAN LIVE FOR DECADES IN A PLACE AND NEVER BECOME A
citizen. Only by going all the way through the citizenship ini-
tiation process can you become a citizen. For your part as a
citizen, you need to submit to the rules and regulations of the
country's government. For the government's part, it agrees to
take you in and give you powerful entitlements. You can only
become a citizen when the government opts to make an agreement with you.

Behind citizenship lies a covenant—a legal contract or
solemn agreement—between the government and each individual citizen. Citizens, in other words, have a contract with
their government. That citizenship covenant gives you so
much power that you can even attack the government. Governments know this, which is one of the reasons they do not

give citizenship to everybody who walks by the immigration office. Citizenship is the most powerful gift, to use the term broadly, that a government can give an individual. The constitution of the government guarantees every citizen has access to the same rights.

Citizens must maintain their access to those rights by complying with a common set of laws. When you move to another country, you do not take your own laws with you. You must submit to that country's laws day in and day out if you expect to carry out your part of the bargain. All covenants or contracts have two parties, and the contract of citizenship is no exception. The citizen's part of the agreement is to comply with the law of the land.

God's Word, the Scriptures, is the Kingdom's
Constitution that guarantees your rights as a citizen.

29

RESPONSIBILITY AND ACCOUNTABILITY

*If anyone sins and does what is forbidden in
any of the Lord's commands, even though they
do not know it, they are guilty and will be
held responsible* (Leviticus 5:17 NIV).

As a citizen, your rights are guaranteed. You do not
have to beg for them. You do not have to bribe anybody to
manipulate favor. When you become a citizen of a country,
you are responsible to that government to follow the laws. The
government is responsible for protecting your rights, but you
always remain accountable for your behavior. If you trans-
gress, you may find yourself deprived of some of your rights
for a while. When people go to prison, their citizenship does
not get revoked, but some of the rights and privileges do—
because they did not hold up their side of the contract as
law-abiding citizens.

A government could give you a piece of property, and it would not be as secure as citizenship because they could take it back and expel you.

In a very real way, citizenship is power-sharing. A citizen shares the power of the government. Essentially, a citizen becomes one with the government. (A negative example of this power would be when an elected government suddenly extends citizenship to a group of people who will then vote them back into power.)

It's important to take King God's commands seriously as a citizen of His Kingdom to maintain all your rights and privileges.

30

An Honor

*David praised the Lord in the presence of the
whole assembly, saying, "...Wealth and honor come
from you; you are the ruler of all things. In your
hands are strength and power to exalt and give
strength to all"* (1 Chronicles 29:10,12 NIV).

No greater honor can be bestowed on an individual
than the honor of citizenship. They could give you a five-year
work permit and yet you would not be able to exercise the
rights of citizenship—and at any time during that five years,
they could change their minds, write a new law, and tell you to
go home immediately.

Citizenship is a privilege, after all. You can't just have it for
the asking. Citizenship is not a right; it is a privilege that gives
you rights. You cannot demand it and you cannot hurry it up.
I have spoken with people who have lived in the Bahamas for
years and who have applied for citizenship, but they are still
waiting. National policy varies from place to place, but the only

quick way to become a citizen is to be born into it, either to be born within the borders of the particular country, or to be born elsewhere to parents who are legal citizens. Some people think it is just a piece of paper that has been stamped by the immigration office. It is a lot more than that. It is a piece of the country.

Citizenship is the conferring of a nation on an individual. They take the whole country and they put it on top of you. You walk in with nothing and you leave with everything on you.

Citizenship in the Kingdom of God is the ultimate honor!

31

FROM DAY ONE

*For God says, "At just the right time, I heard
you. On the day of salvation, I helped you."
Indeed, the "right time" is now. Today is the day
of salvation* (2 Corinthians 6:2 NLT).

ONCE YOU ARE A CITIZEN, YOU CAN OBTAIN A PASSPORT THAT
says so, and people will have to respect your citizenship everywhere you go because you have the whole power of your
government behind you. As a matter of fact, your passport
belongs to the government, not to you personally. It's a crime
to deface it, and you have to surrender it if the government tells
you to do so.

When an official asks to see your passport, that is the single
confirmation of your citizenship. He does not want your birth
certificate or your driver's license. Your passport tells him that
you are a citizen. In most cases, he will ask you a few questions
about what you intend to do in his country, and then he will

stamp it and wave you through. That passport means that he has to treat you right.

On my passport, I read: "Allow the bearer of this document to pass freely without let or hindrance and afford the bearer such assistance and protection as may be necessary." When I return to the country of my citizenship, my passport allows me in without any problem.

My citizenship goes with me wherever I go. I do not have to go to my country or stay in my country to be a citizen. You may not be able to drive a car or vote in an election until you reach a certain age, but you will be considered a citizen from day one of your life.

From the day you accept Jesus Christ as your Lord and Savior, you become a citizen of the Kingdom of God and Heaven. Hallelujah!

32

ENTER INTO YOUR CITIZENSHIP

God decided in advance to adopt us into his own family by bringing us to himself through Jesus Christ. This is what he wanted to do, and it gave him great pleasure (Ephesians 1:5 NLT).

MUCH OF WHAT IT MEANS TO BE A CITIZEN WILL BE A NATURAL part of your life. But sometimes you can appreciate and appropriate more of the benefits of your citizenship by thinking about what it means to enter into it. Here are a few ways you can enter more fully into the already-full citizenship you possess:

Experience it right now. You do not have to wait until you are older and you do not have to visit the capital city. If you are a citizen living in a colony, you do not have to wait until you can travel to the country that colonized your region. You can experience your citizenship right where you are. Explore your citizenship. Just becoming a citizen does not mean you know everything about your country or its freedoms and restrictions. If you are a citizen of the United States, you have fifty states and the District of Columbia to explore. You have more than 300,000 people to meet, different languages to learn, different foods to taste. You could spend the rest of your life exploring your country.

Apply your rights. Lay hold of the benefits and ask for the protections. Enjoy what belongs to you. Being a citizen who does not know his or her rights is like being a non-citizen. Live in the culture where you are a citizen. Embrace more of it. Live a lifestyle that befits a citizen of your country. Submit to the constitutional laws and codes of conduct of your nation. Not only will you stay out of trouble, you will reinforce your claim on the rights and benefits that are yours by virtue of your citizenship status.

Entering into your Kingdom citizenship includes experiencing and exploring God's Word, applying God's rights and promises, living wholeheartedly for Him, and submitting to Kingdom laws and codes of conduct.

33

Dual Citizenship

But they were looking for a better place, a heavenly homeland. That is why God is not ashamed to be called their God, for he has prepared a city for them (Hebrews 11:16 NLT).

Two thousand years ago, when people asked Jesus, "Where are you from?" His answer was that He came from Heaven. His point was that He was not from the earth as they were. He happened to be living on the planet Earth, but His citizenship was in another country—Heaven.

As He explained what He was talking about, people began to understand that He was inviting them to claim heavenly citizenship too. In fact, if they agreed to become "colonists," as I described, they would obtain that heavenly citizenship automatically. At the same time, the only practical thing to do would be to retain their citizenship within a country or kingdom on earth, because that is where they lived and worked and bore their children. So they would need to carry dual citizenship for the rest of their earthly lives.

That invitation still holds. You and I may be very clear in our minds about what country we belong to. But as we learn about the heavenly Kingdom—and how it comes with our heavenly citizenship—we too will carry dual citizenship, if not triple citizenship as in the case of my friends who already have two earthly citizenships to their name. You will adapt to overlapping cultures, but you will throw down your anchor in the place where you see the most promise.

Throw down your anchor in the Kingdom of God—where there is the most and best promise!

34

YOUR SECURE FUTURE

Everything has already been decided. It was known long ago what each person would be. So there's no use arguing with God about your destiny (Ecclesiastes 6:10 NLT).

PAUL WAS ONE OF THE MOST VOCAL EXPOSITORS OF THE promises of the Kingdom of God. In the years after the crucifixion of Jesus, Paul explained the Kingdom of God from one side of the Mediterranean Sea to the other. He wrote a letter to a group of believers in a region that is part of northern Greece today. He was trying to help them deal with persecution from their Roman rulers. The most helpful was to remind them that they did not need to cope with the persecution by using the same reference points—in other words, conflicts between earthly citizenship rights—because in fact our *citizenship is in heaven* (Philippians 3:20 NKJV).

The Kingdom economy is never affected by anything on earth. Remember, all of the power of Heaven is working in our favor. Your future is secure—and so is your present. Dual citizenship is particularly powerful when it is both earthly and divine at the same time. The colonization effort of the Kingdom God is designed to bring Kingdom citizens the advantage of dual citizenship, because the earthly citizenship we start out with cannot protect us. The Kingdom economy is never affected by anything, and all the power of Heaven is working in our favor. Your future is secure—and so is your present. None of it depends on what happens in this world, good or bad, only on what happens in Heaven. In Heaven, everything is always okay.

Just like any earthly citizenship, heavenly citizenship is safeguarded. Under the covering of your heavenly citizenship, you can avoid the contentiousness that comes from the kingdom of darkness. When you learn to prioritize your Kingdom citizenship, you are in a win-win situation every time.

All of Heaven's power is working in your favor.

35

PURE, NOT TAINTED

For out of the heart come evil thoughts—
murder, adultery, sexual immorality, theft, false
testimony, slander (Matthew 15:19 NIV).

IF YOU CHOOSE TO BECOME A CITIZEN OF THE KINGDOM OF
Heaven, inevitably you will hold dual citizenship, whether or
not you recognize the fact. All earthly citizenships, even the
ones that supply excellent benefits and protections, are tainted
by the kingdom of darkness. How could it be otherwise? But
once you hold dual citizenship, you can give preference to the
Kingdom of Light, and I guarantee that you will not regret it.

Most Christians are not in the Kingdom. I know that is a
shocking statement. Members of other religions are not either.
That is because most people who identify themselves as members of a Christian church have remained *citizens* of the same
kingdom of darkness as the people around them. As such, they
can only rise to the level of the jurisdiction under which they
live. Their lifestyle does not change. They may attend meetings

at a church, but they are not as "born again" as they may think they are. Some sing on Sunday and cuss on Monday. That's the way it goes.

They do not carry dual citizenship. They cannot give preference to a superior citizenship, because they don't know about it and they have not sought it out. They do not reflect the culture of the Kingdom, which is a culture of light, freedom from conflict, and much more.

Do you have dual citizenship? Do you reflect the culture of God's Kingdom?

36

A Culture, Not Rituals

They feared the Lord, yet served their own gods—according to the rituals of the nations from among whom they were carried away. To this day they continue practicing the former rituals; they do not fear the Lord, nor do they follow their statutes or their ordinances, or the law and commandment which the Lord had commanded (2 Kings 17:33-34 NKJV).

CITIZENSHIP IN THE KINGDOM IMMERSES YOU IN A CULTURE, not a collection of rituals. That is hard to get across, because we were born into a collection of rituals. Every organized religion, even the simplest ones, have them. They have meetings and procedures and programs and customs and fees; it is all worked out. Every weekend the religions crank up their rituals. (Most of the Christians hold their meetings on Sundays. The Seventh-Day Adventists and the Jews hold theirs on

Saturdays. The Muslims hold theirs on Fridays. Each has their special days.)

Remember, you can't "practice" citizenship. Not only can you not practice and rehearse for citizenship, you can't claim citizenship because you practice and perform various rituals. You can practice a performance or a religion, but never citizenship.

You can't "do" a country like you do a ritual. Think about it. How many times are you a citizen? At what time of day? For how long? Only on the weekend for an hour? Only when you are using a certain language or eating certain foods? Nonsense.

You just *are* a citizen, aren't you? If all the lights go out, you are still a citizen. If you don't pay your taxes or your tithes, you are still a citizen. You may be an irresponsible citizen, but you are still a citizen no matter where you go. And if you are a Kingdom citizen in good standing with your King, you will go far.

Immerse yourself into Kingdom culture
and you will be showered with blessings.

37

THE KINGDOM WITHIN YOU

*And when he [Jesus] was demanded of the
Pharisees, when the kingdom of God should come,
he answered them and said, The kingdom of God
cometh not with observation: Neither shall they
say, Lo here! or, lo there! for, behold, the kingdom
of God is within you* (Luke 17:20-21 KJV).

I HAVE FOUND THAT THE BIBLE EXPLAINS EVERYTHING
better than I can explain it. Here is a good place to pull out a
few lines to explain how the culture of Kingdom citizenship is
completely different from any other culture:

*Now when He was asked by the Pharisees when the
kingdom of God would come, He answered them and
said, "The kingdom of God does not come with observation; nor will they say, 'See here!' or 'See there!'
For indeed, the kingdom of God is within you"*
(Luke 17:20-21 NKJV).

The wind blows where it wishes, and you hear the sound of it, but cannot tell where it comes from and where it goes. So is everyone who is born of the Spirit (John 3:8 NKJV).

When they talk about the Kingdom, people don't say, "There it is, over there!" They can't say that because, like any citizenship, it is invisible, although it makes a noticeable difference in its citizens. It is incorporated inside of its citizens.

What are some ways you can recognize that someone is a Kingdom citizen?

38

TRANSFORMED

Don't copy the behavior and customs of this world,
but let God transform you into a new person by
changing the way you think. Then you will learn
to know God's will for you, which is good and
pleasing and perfect (Romans 12:2 NLT).

PEOPLE CAN DETECT A CERTAIN ESSENCE OF ITS PRESENCE, but it is almost like noticing the way the wind shakes a leaf. To a new citizen of the Kingdom, they may say, "Hey, what's different about you? You don't go with us to the club anymore until the wee hours. You carry yourself differently. You even drive differently. What happened to you?"

This Kingdom causes you to rearrange the furniture inside you, and you don't want to put it back the way it used to be. You become almost like a country within a country—a dual citizen, for a fact.

Every time I go to Los Angeles, I always ask my host to please take me to Chinatown because I like Chinese food. We enter Chinatown through an amazing gate with a dragon on it. Once through the gate, it is as though you are in China. The signs are in Chinese. The people are Chinese. The conversation is conducted in Chinese. You would never go there for pizza, and you would not ask for directions to the nearest McDonald's. When you go to Chinatown, you know what to expect, and you don't expect it to be the same as the rest of the American city outside the gate.

Similarly, as a citizen of the Kingdom you should be distinctive. You begin to forget how to speak the same language as the country you used to be part of. That is why your old friends know they can't use dirty words around you anymore, or gossip, or persuade you to tell a lie. Something has changed, and it's your citizenship. After a while, the people around you will learn what to expect.

Have people noticed that you been transformed from a worldly citizen to a Kingdom citizen?

39

I Am a Kingdom Citizen

May these words of my mouth and this meditation
of my heart be pleasing in your sight, Lord, my
Rock and my Redeemer (Psalm 19:14 NIV).

CITIZENSHIP IS NOT EASILY OBSERVABLE. IT CAN BE HARD TO detect. Sometimes people can't tell until you open your mouth. Then it may be obvious—either your speech is laudable or despicable.

When we are away from home for a long time, living in another country, we pick up the local culture. When we return home, people can figure out that we have been someplace else. We have picked up new vocabulary, and our daily routines have changed.

The same thing happens when you join the Army or any of the armed services. As long as you are part of the armed forces, you are a member of the military, you are no longer a civilian. You must follow a stringent set of rules, even down to what kind of belt and shoes you wear. If your commanding officer says "Jump!" you jump. People who return to civilian life after a long stretch in the military sometimes have an adjustment problem. Outside, everything is different. Inside, they still feel like they are living within the gates of the military complex.

When we become citizens of the Kingdom of Heaven, we have some learning—and un-learning—to do. We have been away from Home so long we think we are earthlings and we have picked up an earthly culture. That is why Kingdom citizens need to pray, *"Thy Kingdom come, thy will be done, on earth as it is in Heaven"*—to fully immerse ourselves into Kingdom culture.

Jump heart and head first into Kingdom culture so your speech and lifestyle reveal you're a heavenling.

40

REPRESENTING GOD'S KINGDOM

*These were the men counted by Moses and
Aaron and the twelve leaders of Israel, each one
representing his family* (Numbers 1:44 NIV).

A KINGDOM CITIZEN IS ONE OF HEAVEN'S REPS, AND HE OR she needs to represent that country everywhere and anywhere. Kingdom citizenship has been conferred upon them. The Son of the King explained it like this: *"I confer on you a kingdom, just as my Father conferred one on me"* (Luke 22:29 NIV). As a Kingdom citizen, not only do you represent the culture, you carry the King's authority with you. This makes a big difference in the way you conduct yourself. A whole country has been conferred upon you.

That means that when you go to work in the morning, Heaven goes with you. Heaven drives your car down the highway. Heaven stops at a gas station to buy fuel. How does

Heaven act under pressure? If someone cuts you off in traffic, how does Heaven respond?

These are the real issues of citizenship, and you will deal with them every day. Do you represent your country properly? Representing your country is part of your corporate responsibility. People will be watching you, and because of you, they will decide what they think of the King and His Kingdom. Make sure you have not been away from home for so long (so to speak) that you have picked up the local culture.

People from earth have their minds on earthly things (see Philippians 3:19). Their minds reflect the culture around them. They try to solve their problems from the perspective of those people and culture. They don't have the advantage of calling on the wisdom and stability and wealth of the Kingdom of Heaven. They may not even know that is an option.

Make sure you have not been away from home for
so long that you have picked up the local culture.

41

FIRST CHOICE

But seek first his kingdom and his righteousness,
and all these things will be given to you
as well (Matthew 6:33 NIV).

I TOLD YOU ABOUT MY FRIENDS WHO HAVE DUAL CITIZENSHIP. With dual citizenship, they have a contingency plan. If things don't work out in the country on one side of the ocean, they can move back to the other country.

I caution you not to live as if you have declared independence from Heaven. You want to hang on to the dual citizenship, and you want to give preference to the Kingdom regardless of what continent or island you may be living on. The currency of the Kingdom of Heaven can be used in any country on the face of the earth, because it is called love. The educational system keeps you on top of things at all times, because you never stop learning. The social service system is so good it is beyond description.

I made my Kingdom citizenship my first choice a long time ago, and I hope you do too. I assure you that you will never find a better kind of citizenship anywhere. Keep reading to find out how to become a citizen of the Kingdom of Heaven, if you are not already one, and how to enjoy fully the privileges and advantages of that citizenship wherever you may go on earth.

When thinking about your priorities, is your Kingdom citizenship at the top of the list?

42

JESUS AND THE KINGDOM

But the crowds found out where he was going, and they followed him. He [Jesus] welcomed them and taught them about the Kingdom of God, and he healed those who were sick (Luke 9:11 NLT).

EVERYBODY IN THE WORLD KNOWS WHAT JESUS DID TWO thousand years ago, even the pagans. The atheists know what He did. The Muslims and the Hindus know too, whether they believe it or not. When Jesus died on that bloody Roman cross outside the city of Jerusalem, crucified, His death rocked the foundations of human culture so deeply that they have never stopped reverberating.

His death is so well-known because He did not stay dead for long. You cannot kill the King of Heaven, as people discovered when He rose from the dead after three days in the grave. As a matter of fact, this King is the most unique king in human history, because He is still alive, and His Kingdom is too.

Although everybody knows what Jesus did, relatively few people—and this includes Christians, the ones who talk the most about Jesus—know what He stands for. They have not perceived the fact that when Jesus was working and teaching in Jerusalem and in the towns all up and down the countryside, His primary message was about the Kingdom of Heaven, which was His home country. He talked about the Kingdom all the time, using that very term.

Jesus's primary message was about the Kingdom of Heaven—His home country.

43

JESUS'S HOME COUNTRY

*From that time Jesus began to preach and
to say, "Repent, for the kingdom of heaven
is at hand"* (Matthew 4:17 NKJV).

THE WORD *KINGDOM* IS MENTIONED IN THE NEW TESTAMENT
of the Bible (the part that was written after Jesus was born),
about 160 times. Most of these times, *kingdom* is referring to
the Kingdom of God.

The four books written by Jesus's disciples Matthew, Mark,
Luke, and John are known as the Gospels, and they contain the
firsthand accounts of the events of Jesus's life. The Gospel of
Matthew uses the phrase "Kingdom of Heaven." The authors
of the other three Gospels prefer "Kingdom of God." The two
terms mean the same thing.

So all through Jesus's recorded preaching, the word *kingdom* appears far more often than the other words you might
expect to see, such as *eternal life, born again, forgiveness,* or
love. Jesus talked about the Kingdom all the time. It was His

main topic, His primary reference point. In fact, you would be exactly right if you said that Jesus's whole purpose in coming to earth was to reintroduce the Kingdom of Heaven to a world that had completely lost track of the truth about it.

Should Christians refer to their home country as the Kingdom of God? Do you?

44

SON OF GOD, SON OF MAN, KING OF ISRAEL

Nathanael answered and said to Him,
"Rabbi, You are the Son of God! You are the
King of Israel!" (John 1:49 NKJV)

No one has gone up into heaven, but there is One who
came down from heaven, the Son of Man [Himself—
whose home is in heaven] (John 3:13 AMP).

YOU COULD SAY THAT JESUS CHRIST IS THE MOST MISUN-derstood person on earth, because even His closest followers, the Christians (the people who carry His name), have misconstrued His message. I would go so far as to call it a tragedy that we have produced a religion called Christianity. Jesus Christ did not invent such a thing. Even in the Bible stories about Him and about the undertakings of His disciples, the word *Christian* is used only twice, and one of them is derogatory.

It is time to set things straight. Jesus did not come to set up a religion. He came to establish an outpost of the Kingdom of Heaven.

Jesus did not exercise His right to become a teacher until He was thirty years old. Then for the next three years, He roamed the countryside as an itinerant rabbi, teaching anyone who would listen what the Kingdom was like and demonstrating its liberating power with miraculous signs.

A good part of His message was "repent"—change your thinking. Change your thinking to what? To Kingdom thinking, to a recognition of heavenly lordship.

In the finest definition, Christianity isn't
a religion—so how would you define it?

45

JESUS'S KINGDOM TEACHINGS

From that time Jesus began to preach and say, "Repent [change your inner self—your old way of thinking, regret past sins, live your life in a way that proves repentance; seek God's purpose for your life], for the kingdom of heaven is at hand" (Matthew 4:17 AMP).

THAT IS WHAT JESUS SAID IN THE FIRST RECORDED WORDS OF His teaching:

From that time [immediately after His baptism and forty days in the wilderness] *Jesus began to preach and to say, "Repent, for the kingdom of heaven is at hand"* (Matthew 4:17 NKJV).

From that time on Jesus began to preach, "Repent, for the kingdom of heaven has come near" (Matthew 4:17 NIV).

The words *at hand* and *near* mean the same thing. The Kingdom was approaching, and Jesus was announcing its coming. As a matter of fact, He was ushering it in. He didn't give people more laws and religious rituals to learn. They had enough of those already. He wanted to tell people what to do with their lives, how to become naturalized—perhaps I should say "supernaturalized"—citizens of the Kingdom of Heaven.

Jesus did not come to set up a religion. He came to establish an outpost of the Kingdom of Heaven.

After He spent three years teaching, preaching, and demonstrating what the Kingdom was like, some people objected to His ideas so much that they plotted to have him killed. You would think that would have taken care of it. Dead men can't preach against your cherished religion, and a man in a tomb can no longer claim to be leading the way to this so-called Kingdom. His opponents especially disliked the fact that He seemed to be claiming some kind of kingship.

Killing Jesus didn't stop His teachings from being spread worldwide for the next 2,000-plus years.

46

EARTH, THE KINGDOM OF HEAVEN OUTPOST

Then God said, "Let us make human beings in our image, to be like us. They will reign over the fish in the sea, the birds in the sky, the livestock, all the wild animals on the earth, and the small animals that scurry along the ground." So God created human beings in his own image. In the image of God he created them; male and female he created them (Genesis 1:26-27 NLT).

JESUS'S DEATH AND SUBSEQUENT RESURRECTION COMPLETED the purpose of His mission to earth—to re-establish a Kingdom outpost among the people who lived under the human jurisdictions of the world, to reclaim the territory of earth for the Kingdom of Heaven.

Originally, the Kingdom of Heaven had established an outpost in a place that people know as the Garden of Eden. Here is how the first book of the Bible describes it:

> *Then God said, "Let Us make man in Our image,
> according to Our likeness; let them have domin-
> ion over the fish of the sea, over the birds of the air,
> and over the cattle, over all the earth and over every
> creeping thing that creeps on the earth." So God cre-
> ated man in His own image; in the image of God
> He created him; male and female He created them*
> (Genesis 1:26-27 NKJV).

"Let them have dominion," God said. The word used in the original Hebrew is *mamlakah,* which is the same word that gets translated into English as "kingdom." It also gets translated as "reign," "sovereignty," and "realm." So dominion is the same as kingdom. You can see the "dom" syllable in both words because the words *dominion* and *kingdom* are closely related.

All of these words indicate that someone is in charge of something. Having dominion means having authority over. It means reigning, leading, managing, ruling over. According to the account in Genesis, human beings were created to manage the rest of creation. We can see this throughout the rest of the story about the first man and woman, and on through all of human history up to the present day.

King God was assigning dominion to the people He had created. What were the people supposed to have dominion over? Their assignment on earth was to manage the real estate He had created as an extension of His rule in Heaven. First He created the earth and all the living things that fill it, and then the King brought Heaven to earth and set up His gov-ernment, His system of management.

God created humans with the intention of having them represent His authority on the planet He had created.

47

MANAGEMENT FAILURE

*But the Lord God warned him, "You may freely eat
the fruit of every tree in the garden—except the tree
of the knowledge of good and evil. If you eat its fruit,
you are sure to die" (Genesis 2:16-17 NLT).*

As managers of the outpost of the Kingdom of Heaven,
Adam and Eve had only one restriction: do not eat the fruit
from that particular tree. That one rule was evidently very
important to God, because He told them that breaking it
would mean death. But a wily serpent came along and con-
tradicted what God had said. Adam's wife Eve believed the
serpent's lie, and she took a bite, offering some to her husband
as well. God confronted them:

> *Then to Adam He said, "Because you have heeded
> the voice of your wife, and have eaten from the tree
> of which I commanded you, saying, 'You shall not eat
> of it': Cursed is the ground for your sake; in toil you
> shall eat of it all the days of your life. Both thorns*

and thistles it shall bring forth for you, and you shall eat the herb of the field. In the sweat of your face you shall eat bread till you return to the ground, for out of it you were taken; for dust you are, and to dust you shall return." ...*Therefore the Lord God sent him out of the garden of Eden to till the ground from which he was taken. So He drove out the man* (Genesis 3:17-19, 23-24 NKJV).

No longer could the Kingdom of Heaven claim to have an outpost on earth. God had created the humans to represent His authority and exercise dominion for Him. They failed. We call it the Fall. This is the declaration of independence described previously. The colonists had ruptured their relationship with their King, and they could not repair it. The only way the colony could be re-established would have to involve the King's Son, Jesus.

Only the King's Son could repair
the relationship—and Jesus did!

48

A Child Is Born

For there is born to you this day in the city of David a Savior, who is Christ the Lord (Luke 2:11 NKJV).

MANY GENERATIONS OF PEOPLE LIVED AND DIED IN THE meantime before Jesus came to earth. Some of them began to expect Him. Religious people talked about it. In the whole region not far from where the first man had failed to manage the first colony of the Kingdom, prophets tried to describe what God was going to do. Some of them got very specific:

> *For unto us a Child is born, unto us a Son is given; and the government will be upon His shoulder. And His name will be called Wonderful, Counselor, Mighty God, Everlasting Father, Prince of Peace. Of the increase of His government and peace there will be no end* (Isaiah 9:6-7 NKJV).

This Child whom the prophet Isaiah was talking about was coming to reestablish the government of Heaven on earth.

He would *not* be coming to set up a better religion, because Adam hadn't lost a religion—he had lost dominion.

When the Son finally did arrive, most people didn't know who He was. They thought He was the firstborn son of a simple carpenter and his wife. They did not understand until later that He was the long-expected Son of God, the "Second Adam," whose life, death, and resurrection would undo the judgment that had been rendered upon Adam so long before.

Even to this day, in spite of centuries of the religion called Christianity, most people don't understand that Jesus makes it possible for them to reengage with God's original plan. They know next to nothing about becoming citizens of the Kingdom Jesus talked so much about, and very little about resuming their role as God's representatives in the territory called earth.

How many of the Christians you know have resumed their role as God's representatives in their workplace, community, church, home?

49

JESUS PREACHED THE KINGDOM

[Jesus said,] *"And this gospel of the kingdom will be preached in the whole world as a testimony to all nations, and then the end will come"* (Matthew 24:14 NIV).

THE NEW TESTAMENT DOCUMENTS JESUS'S NUMEROUS MESsages and teachings about the most unique Kingdom of God and Heaven. Jesus even kept talking about the Kingdom after He rose from the grave: *"After his suffering, he presented himself to them and gave many convincing proofs that he was alive. He appeared to them over a period of forty days and spoke about the kingdom of God"* (Acts 1:3 NIV).

Jesus never stopped talking about the Kingdom. He was careful about referring to Himself as the King, and yet His disciples could tell that He was the One all of the prophets from Joshua to Malachi had been talking about when they announced the coming of a future Messiah. Some of the books in the Old Testament had given details about His lineage (the book of Ruth, for example). Others proclaimed the future coming of an unnamed, magnificent king who would take care of all the injustices that plagued the nation of Israel. Psalmists such as King David provided tantalizing details (see Psalms 22 and 45). The prophet Micah included the name of the village in which Jesus's mother, Mary, would give birth to Him:

> *But you, Bethlehem Ephrathah, though you are little among the thousands of Judah, yet out of you shall come forth to Me the One to be Ruler in Israel, whose goings forth are from of old, from everlasting* (Micah 5:2 NKJV).

As that first man had lost the heavenly assignment for the whole race, the "Second Adam," Jesus, restored it. Now all we have to do is to recognize what He has done and get on board.

So many Scriptures prove positive that Jesus came to reconcile the Kingdom of God and the people of the outpost.

50

KINGDOM PREACHERS

*Therefore, my brothers and sisters, make every effort
to confirm your calling and election. For if you do these
things, you will never stumble, and you will receive
a rich welcome into the eternal kingdom of our Lord
and Savior Jesus Christ* (2 Peter 1:10-11 NIV).

NOT ONLY DID JESUS TALK UNCEASINGLY ABOUT THE KING-
dom, His disciples and others did as well. John (the one we call
John the Baptist because he baptized a lot of people, including Jesus) was Jesus's cousin. He started talking about the
Kingdom before Jesus became known to the public. His was a
prophetic voice and considered a "forerunner" of Jesus:

> *In those days John the Baptist came, preaching in
> the wilderness of Judea and saying, "Repent, for the
> kingdom of heaven has come near." This is he who
> was spoken of through the prophet Isaiah: "A voice
> of one calling in the wilderness, 'Prepare the way for*

the Lord, make straight paths for him'" (Matthew 3:1-3 NIV).

Jesus sent out His first twelve disciples to talk about what it means to be citizens in His Kingdom, and they in turn commissioned all of His other followers to do the same, wherever their paths took them. The following are only a few examples:

> *But when they believed Philip as he preached the things concerning the kingdom of God and the name of Jesus Christ, both men and women were baptized* (Acts 8:12 NKJV).
>
> *And when they had preached the gospel to that city and made many disciples, they returned to Lystra, Iconium, and Antioch, strengthening the souls of the disciples, exhorting them to continue in the faith, and saying, "We must through many tribulations enter the kingdom of God." So when they had appointed elders in every church, and prayed with fasting, they commended them to the Lord in whom they had believed* (Acts 14:21-23 NKJV).
>
> *Listen, my beloved brethren: Has God not chosen the poor of this world to be rich in faith and heirs of the kingdom which He promised to those who love Him?* (James 2:5 NKJV)

Rather than the Kingdom, where is the focus of many pastors today? Why is that?

51

PAUL AND THE KINGDOM

The kingdom of God is not eating and drinking,
but righteousness and peace and joy in the
Holy Spirit (Romans 14:17 NKJV).

PAUL TRAVELED MORE THAN ALL OF THE DISCIPLES, AND HE talked about the Kingdom when he wrote letters to the believers all across the Mediterranean world:

> *Some of you have become arrogant, as if I were not coming to you. But I will come to you very soon, if the Lord is willing, and then I will find out not only how these arrogant people are talking, but what power they have. For the kingdom of God is not a matter of talk but of power* (1 Corinthians 4:18-20 NIV).

> *For our citizenship is in heaven, from which we also eagerly wait for the Savior, the Lord Jesus Christ* (Philippians 3:20 NKJV).

In fact, Paul was so determined to talk about the Kingdom that he once suspended his travels for more than two years in order to talk about it. He was in Ephesus at the time:

> *Paul entered the synagogue and spoke boldly there for three months, arguing persuasively about the kingdom of God. But some of them became obstinate; they refused to believe and publicly maligned the Way. So Paul left them. He took the disciples with him and had discussions daily in the lecture hall of Tyrannus. This went on for two years* (Acts 19:8-10 NIV).

Before this, Paul had always moved on to a new city. He actually stopped traveling for two years in order to stay in the same city and get the Kingdom into the hearts and minds of the people.

Obviously the Kingdom of God and Heaven is vital when spreading the Good News.

52

†††

LOTS TO LEARN
AND TALK ABOUT

Then Paul dwelt two whole years in his own rented
house, and received all who came to him, preaching
the kingdom of God and teaching the things which
concern the Lord Jesus Christ with all confidence,
no one forbidding him (Acts 28:30-31 NKJV).

REMEMBER, THE KINGDOM IS A COUNTRY. YOU CAN'T EXPLAIN
everything about it in thirty minutes. You can't explain everything about the country where you live in that length of time,
either. Paul could not teach enough about the Kingdom in one
sitting. He talked about it for several hours every day for two
years! He was describing the country of Heaven and how it
affects the people on earth. He talked about colonizing the
known world, and about importing the Kingdom constitution
and all of its laws, along with the intricacies of social relations
and cultural expressions.

At the end of his life, Paul restated the fact that he, like Jesus, had preached about one topic, the Kingdom of God: *"And indeed, now I know that you all, among whom I have gone* preaching the kingdom of God, *will see my face no more"* (Acts 20:25 NKJV).

Paul was taken to Rome as a prisoner. A long time passed before he went to trial. What did he do with his time? He taught about the Kingdom, of course:

> *So when they had appointed him a day, many came*
> *to him at his lodging, to whom he explained and sol-*
> *emnly testified of the kingdom of God, persuading*
> *them concerning Jesus from both the Law of Moses*
> *and the Prophets, from morning till evening* (Acts 28:23 NKJV).

Any subject that so dominates the preaching and teaching in the Bible is worth our entire attention.

We must learn about the Kingdom and we
must become citizens as soon as we can.

53

THE SECRET TO LIFE

[Jesus said,] *"The Kingdom of Heaven is like a treasure that a man discovered hidden in a field. In his excitement, he hid it again and sold everything he owned to get enough money to buy the field. Again, the Kingdom of Heaven is like a merchant on the lookout for choice pearls. When he discovered a pearl of great value, he sold everything he owned and bought it!"* (Matthew 13:44-46 NLT)

I WILL PUT IT TO YOU: THE KINGDOM IS THE SECRET TO LIFE. The secret to a full and fulfilled life is the discovery, understanding, and application of the Kingdom of Heaven on earth. You have to learn how the Kingdom works, how to apply what you have learned every day.

Religion keeps you postponing the Kingdom until the future, by and by when you die. It is time to start living in the Kingdom here and now. The Kingdom of God is now. You must enter into citizenship while you are still on earth. Today

I am a citizen, and I experience the full rights and responsibilities of citizenship. The Kingdom is what you're looking for. Your religion isn't enough. The Kingdom of Heaven is like that "pearl of great price" or the treasure hidden in the field that Jesus talked about—something so precious that whoever finds it rushes out to sell everything they own to buy it.

The man who found the treasure and the man who found the pearl sold everything. In the same way, we need to sell everything in order to be "sold out" for the Kingdom. We need to sell all of our old belief systems and previous opinions. Some of us need to sell our theological degrees for the Kingdom. Others need to sell their grandparents' denomination into which they were born. Some need to sell their loyalty to the pastor they love so much but who isn't preaching about the Kingdom. Everything other than the Kingdom needs to go—it pales in comparison to the treasured pearl of the Kingdom.

We need to be "sold out" for the Kingdom.

54

GOD'S GOOD PLEASURE

*Jesus said, "Do not fear, little flock, for it
is your Father's good pleasure to give you
the kingdom"* (Luke 12:32 NKJV).

AS A CHRISTIAN, YOU MAY THINK YOU ALREADY HAVE THE
pearl—until you find the real thing. Humans are collecting all
kinds of pearls, searching for the best one. Some choose Islam;
that is a pearl. Some choose Buddhism; that is a pearl. Some
choose Mormonism. Some choose yoga. Some choose Uni-
tarianism. Some choose atheism. All of those are pearls. Yet!
The minute someone discovers the Kingdom—which is not a
religion even though it may carry the name of Jesus Christ—
they know they have found all that they ever wanted. They can
give up all other pearls.

As a Christian, you may still worry about tomorrow and
fret about the present. As a Kingdom citizen, you can count on
the limitless resources of your heavenly Father as never before.
You may need to learn some things about being a Kingdom

citizen before you can enjoy those resources, but they will be yours for the asking. Jesus said:

> *These things dominate the thoughts of unbelievers all over the world, but your Father already knows your needs. Seek the Kingdom of God above all else, and he will give you everything you need. So don't be afraid, little flock. For it gives your Father great happiness to give you the Kingdom. Sell your possessions and give to those in need. This will store up treasure for you in heaven! And the purses of heaven never get old or develop holes. Your treasure will be safe; no thief can steal it and no moth can destroy it* (Luke 12:30-33 NLT).

As a Kingdom citizen, you can always count on the limitless resources of your heavenly Father.

55

GOD'S BIBLE, GOD'S CONSTITUTION

The earth suffers for the sins of its people, for they have twisted God's instructions, violated his laws, and broken his everlasting covenant (Isaiah 24:5 NLT).

A KING'S WILL, PURPOSE, AND INTENT ARE EXPRESSED IN THE form of laws. Every country has laws, and the Kingdom of Heaven is no exception. The Bible is filled with the laws of God, and that means we can call it the constitution of the Kingdom of God.

When you read the Bible, you come away with a strong impression of "Thy will be done." We call the older part of the Bible the "Old Testament" and the newer part the "New Testament." A testament is simply a documented will, God's will in this case. (Your "last will and testament" is your documented statement about how you wish to distribute your possessions upon death.) The collection of books we call the Bible is filled with the King's ideas and promises about His country and what He wants for His citizens. The Bible is God's Testament.

In a democracy, a constitution comes from the people. In fact, in the United States of America, the first words of the constitution are "We, the people...." The constitution of the Bahamas begins in a similar way. But when a constitution comes from "we, the people," it can be changed by the people. God's constitution, the Bible, will not change.

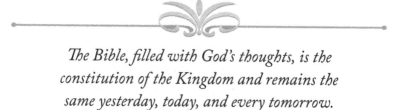

The Bible, filled with God's thoughts, is the constitution of the Kingdom and remains the same yesterday, today, and every tomorrow.

56

KINGDOM ORIENTATION AND ALIGNMENT

Then the King will say to those on his right,
"Come, you who are blessed by my Father; take your
inheritance, the kingdom prepared for you since the
creation of the world" (Matthew 25:34 NIV).

HAVING PRESENTED THE IDEA THAT THE BIBLE IS THE CONstitution of the Kingdom of God, I want to quote a few statements from that Constitution, for the sake of your orientation and alignment with the Kingdom way of doing things. These statements will move you into a thought process. The more you read the Constitution of the Kingdom with a "Kingdom filter" on your mind, the more the light of understanding will dawn for you.

> *Now, therefore, you are no longer strangers and for-*
> *eigners, but fellow citizens with the saints and*
> *members of the household of God* (Ephesians 2:19
> NKJV).

Giving thanks to the Father who has qualified us to be partakers of the inheritance of the saints in the light (Colossians 1:12 NKJV).

For our citizenship is in heaven, from which we also eagerly wait for the Savior, the Lord Jesus Christ (Philippians 3:20 NKJV).

These words in the Constitution of the Kingdom were written to citizens of the Kingdom in the present tense. These rights, privileges, and duties belong to every citizen, including you, even if you are a very new citizen. You cannot earn them or improve on them.

You can, however, remain ignorant of them and ignore them. That is why it is so important to talk about the Kingdom and to keep reading its Constitution in-depth in order to understand it.

Many sections of the Kingdom constitution were written by Paul who spent most of his adult life preaching, teaching, and writing letters to citizens of the Kingdom, helping them adjust to the Kingdom lifestyle. Sometimes the citizens had adjustment problems—social, cultural, relationship, money problems, etc. Paul explained to them, "Look, to live in this Kingdom there are some things you need to do, and some other things you need to stop doing, and here they are."

Turn your thoughts over to the Kingdom King. Let Him reorient your thinking.

57

MISCONCEPTIONS

*But there were also false prophets among the people,
even as there will be false teachers among you, who
will secretly bring in destructive heresies, even
denying the Lord who bought them, and bring on
themselves swift destruction* (2 Peter 2:1 NKJV).

MOST OF OUR ADJUSTMENT PROBLEMS START IN OUR HEADS.
Therefore, we need a mental transformation if we want to
become full citizens of the Kingdom. We need to figure out
our misconceptions and how to get rid of them, especially religious concepts we have heard all our lives. You and I want to
be citizens of the Kingdom, free from labels and assumptions.
I don't want to be Baptist, Methodist, Episcopalian, Catholic,
Seventh-Day Adventist, Church of God, Assemblies of God,
charismatic, or Pentecostal anymore. I don't want to think of
myself as a businessman, a pastor, an advisor, or any other kind
of career person.

I want misconceptions to be carefully and continually cleaned out of me so I can start over. I want to start fresh as a citizen of the Kingdom of God. And I want you to start fresh, too, looking for the next assignment He will give you.

Turn over all of your possessions to Him, your King—He owns it all anyway. Let Him show you how to redistribute everything you thought you owned. Build your life on the Bible, the Constitution of the Kingdom of God and Heaven. Allow it to become a way of life, a lifestyle that honors God and gives Him glory.

Beware of false teachers and
misconceptions that pervert God's Word.

58

NOISE

Or they mouth empty, boastful words and, by appealing to the lustful desires of the flesh, they entice people who are just escaping from those who live in error (2 Peter 2:18 NIV).

ANYONE WHO HAS STUDIED COMMUNICATIONS KNOWS WHAT I mean when I say "noise." A sender sends a message to an intended receiver, and noise is what happens during the transmission, in between when the message leaves the sender and gets received by the recipient. The noise can be very complicated to understand because it includes your culture, your educational level, your social upbringing, your religious history, your values, your moral status, and your present situation in life.

A lot of "noise" is hidden and silent. The most important part of noise is what I call "concept"—an idea, a thought conceived as a mental picture. Thoughts are very powerful, even the ones that are never expressed in words. A word is an exposed thought, but most thoughts never get expressed. We think first, then we speak or write. We try to express our thoughts and we want others to understand them—but their own thoughts often alter their comprehension, resulting in misunderstandings or misconceptions.

Misconceptions are dangerous. Marriages can break up because of them. Governments and churches break up because of misconceptions too. If you build your whole life on a certain idea and it becomes theory and then philosophy and then doctrine and then a belief system and finally a way of life and a mentality, you will not know that you have basically built your life on a lie. To you, it is not a lie; it's the truth, and you will strongly defend even your misconception.

Avoid misconceptions by fully focusing on
God's Word—filled with truth and freedom.

59

PRE-EXISTING CONCEPTS

*Because, although they knew God, they did not
glorify Him as God, nor were thankful, but
became futile in their thoughts, and their foolish
hearts were darkened* (Romans 1:21 NKJV).

WHEN IT COMES TO TRUTH ABOUT YOU AND GOD, MOST
likely much of what you believe has been contaminated. People
interpret words about God through their preexisting concepts.
This includes the words in the Bible. Your seminary degree
could be contaminated with ignorance of the true concepts
about God. You and your pastor and your church friends could
all have pieces of the truth, but none of you has asked the original Sender to clear your mind of contaminated concepts so you
can get the message right.

The King anticipated this problem. This is why He provided an expert Counselor for us—the Holy Spirit—who can
personally help you capture the correct concepts that come to

you from the mind of God. *"He will guide you into all truth,"* said Jesus's disciple John (John 16:13).

Correct concepts about God include truth about the Kingdom of God. When you rediscover the truth about your Kingdom citizenship, you rediscover something that has been lost over the years. The average person living in the Western world has no real understanding of the words that Jesus used. So we superimpose on His words our concepts, which come from our culture and our environment. We build our lives on our own conclusions and we create a belief system called religion.

Instead of reading out of the Bible, we read into the Bible. And we miss the Kingdom because of the noise in our heads.

60

REMEDY FOR NOISE

*Jesus said, "I assure you and most solemnly say
to you, unless you repent [that is, change your
inner self—your old way of thinking, live
changed lives] and become like children [trusting,
humble, and forgiving], you will never enter the
kingdom of heaven"* (Matthew 18:3 AMP).

JESUS HAD THE PERFECT REMEDY FOR NOISE. HE HELD A
child in front of His disciples and said, *"Truly I tell you, unless
you change and become like little children, you will never enter the
kingdom of heaven"* (Matthew 18:3 NIV). Entering the Kingdom requires that you exchange your theology, your doctrine,
your old religion, and your independent self-sufficiency for
something new. Unless you change, you can't enter.

When a rich young man asked Jesus how he could be sure
he would go to the Kingdom of Heaven, Jesus answered, "Keep
the commandments," in other words, "Obey the laws of the
country of Heaven" (see Matthew 19:16-30). But the young

man was rich in material possessions. He had obeyed the law, but he was not humble. So Jesus said, "*Truly I tell you, it is hard for someone who is rich to enter the kingdom of heaven*" (Matthew 19:23 NIV). The young man was so used to making his own living that it was difficult to let the King do it. He had been schooled in self-sufficiency; it was tough to believe that God could supply his needs. His good life was getting in the way of Kingdom life.

In a way, we are like that rich young ruler. Our noisy theology and concepts occupy our minds and hearts. Not only do we need to listen to Jesus about becoming like children, we need to remember the first words of His public ministry, "*Repent, for the kingdom of heaven is at hand*" (Matthew 4:17 NKJV).

The Kingdom has arrived. It is here already. If you don't change your thinking in time, you will miss it.

61

PURE PROVISION

For if, by the trespass of the one man, death reigned
through that one man, how much more will those
who receive God's abundant provision of grace and
of the gift of righteousness reign in life through the
one man, Jesus Christ! (Romans 5:17 NIV)

IF YOU SEEK THE KINGDOM OF HEAVEN AND ITS KING, YOU
will not have to worry about anything else—riches or poverty,
sickness or health, life or death. In seeking the Kingdom, you
are also seeking—and you will find—the pure provision of
the King.

Jesus said, "*Therefore do not worry, saying, 'What shall we*
eat?' or 'What shall we drink?' or 'What shall we wear?'...For
your heavenly Father knows that you need all these things. But seek
first the kingdom of God and His righteousness, and all these things
shall be added to you" (Matthew 6:31-33 NKJV).

Another time, Jesus made it clear that anybody who seeks
for righteousness will surely find it: "*Blessed are those who*

hunger and thirst for righteousness, for they shall be filled" (Matthew 5:6 NKJV). Once you find the Kingdom, you also find righteousness. Your religious friends may not understand the change that has happened. Nevertheless, you will have found what you were looking for, and you will want to hang on to it.

In my experience, once people really know about the true Kingdom of God and they see it modeled, they want to get in. Citizenship in the Kingdom is a powerful lure. Most pastors do not understand the Kingdom so they do not preach it or teach it. Consequently, most people in the churches have not entered into the Kingdom, and they can't model it. Why should it be a surprise that nobody wants to join their church? What is surprising is that anybody does.

*When seeking the Kingdom, you will find the
King's pure provision for every contingency of life.*

62

NEW BIRTH

*But first and most importantly seek (aim at,
strive after) His kingdom and His righteousness
[His way of doing and being right—the attitude
and character of God], and all these things will
be given to you also* (Matthew 6:33 AMP).

SEEKING THE KINGDOM MEANS SEEKING NATURALIZED CITIzenship in the Kingdom of Light. This is a completely new orientation for most of us. Once we attain citizenship, others will want to join us as immigrants, leaving behind the kingdom of darkness.

We enter Kingdom citizenship through "new birth." Many people call this being saved, but in terms of the Kingdom orientation, I think it is more helpful to think of it as birth. We call it being born again, and it is the same as changing your mind from rebellion to submission to the government of God.

When we seek to become citizens of God's Kingdom, we voluntarily align ourselves with a new government and a new country. We embrace its language, its ideals, and its values. A Kingdom lifestyle is typified by humility and prosperity at the same time, which is an appealing combination to the non-citizens around us.

And like any children, we are born into the line of inheritance that our Father has established. Everything in the Kingdom is inherited just by being born. Starting the moment you step into the Kingdom, it is as if you have a blank check in your hand at all times. You can't go off to a beautiful island and retire from the affairs of normal life, but inside your mind and emotions, you will feel that way—as your King will start taking care of your needs. That includes your need to have a fulfilling and meaningful life!

New birth naturalizes us to our original state of exercising authority and dominion over the earth, when the King takes care of all our needs.

63

FREE AND SECURE

*Now the Lord is the Spirit, and where the Spirit
of the Lord is, there is liberty [emancipation from
bondage, true freedom]* (2 Corinthians 3:17 AMP).

IN THE KINGDOM, YOU AND YOUR POSSESSIONS DO NOT NEED
protection. Before you are a citizen in God's Kingdom, when
you accumulate stuff you worry about it being stolen and may
even put in a security system. But the Kingdom offers freedom.
Changing your mind and surrendering everything to the King
brings you into a whole new place. That is why Jesus said:

> *Do not lay up for yourselves treasures on earth,
> where moth and rust destroy and where thieves
> break in and steal; but lay up for yourselves trea-
> sures in heaven, where neither moth nor rust destroys
> and where thieves do not break in and steal. For
> where your treasure is, there your heart will be also*
> (Matthew 6:19-21 NKJV).

Crime is impossible in Heaven, where there is no private ownership. No one can rob you anymore. Inflation and destruction can't get to the treasures you have laid up in Heaven, either. Your life is free from stress. Whenever you lack something in your life, the King of Heaven furnishes it for you.

You may live on earth in a colony of the Kingdom of Heaven, but you remain a full citizen of the Kingdom of God.

64

ADAMIC CITIZENSHIP RESTORED

Finally, brothers and sisters, rejoice! Strive for full restoration, encourage one another, be of one mind, live in peace. And the God of love and peace will be with you (2 Corinthians 13:11 NIV).

WE KNOW THAT THE FIRST KINGDOM IN EXISTENCE WAS THE Kingdom of Heaven. There was no kingdom before that one. And the very first citizen of the colony of the Kingdom of Heaven on earth was the very first man, Adam. God took some dirt and formed Adam's body, and then He breathed the Spirit into the body. Each of us is like the first man, Adam; we have a body that comes from the earth and a spirit that comes from God.

God never intended that Adam, or any of us, would be considered citizens of earth, or even permanent residents. Adamic citizenship refers to a continuation of God's original plan. Where is our citizenship? Heaven. Do we expect to gain that citizenship status only upon arriving in Heaven after our death? Is it like retirement? Or can we experience heavenly citizenship right now? You know the answer by now. No matter where you go, your citizenship stays the same—you remain a full citizen of Heaven.

But some of us have become so used to earth that we can't imagine our home country as anywhere else. Some even become a little afraid of the very country we are supposed to rule. Jesus was never intimidated by anything, whether it was a storm, or demons, or strong wind, or pestilence. He knew He was above all that. And we should have that mindset as well.

Remember, "When Jesus had called the Twelve together, he gave them power and authority to drive out all demons and to cure diseases, and he sent them out to proclaim the kingdom of God and to heal the sick" (Luke 9:1-2 NIV).

65

SUPERMAN JESUS

*Jesus came and told his disciples, "I have
been given all authority in heaven and
on earth"* (Matthew 28:18 NLT).

IT WOULD NOT BE DISRESPECTFUL TO SAY JESUS IS LIKE SUPER-
man. He came from another planet, so to speak, and when He
got here, He had super powers. As a matter of fact, the Super-
man story is probably the closest story to explain who you are.
You, too, are from another "planet," Heaven. When you came
here, your powers kicked in because your only dominion is on
earth. When you go back to Heaven, you will not need your
powers anymore. Kryptonite is sin. When you disobey God's
laws, you lose your powers on earth. Obedience protects you
from kryptonite. It is that simple.

Adam was the first citizen from Heaven on earth, and he
was given all the rights, privileges, and authority of the heavenly kingdom, so that he could exercise dominion over the
earth. God gave Adam authority over the fish of the sea, the

birds of the air, the cattle of the field, the creatures that creep over the ground—over all the earth.

We are supposed to be part of that same arrangement. We are from Heaven, and we live on the earth, having brought all of Heaven's authority with us. For most of us to remember that we are really citizens of Heaven takes a major reorientation. Next time you walk into a meeting, engage in some kind of negotiations, or interview for a job, fix your mind on your true citizenship. "I'm not from here," you can say to yourself. "When I walk into a room, my King walks in too. Through me, He is in charge here."

As a citizen of the Kingdom of God and Heaven, I represent my heavenly Father in all I do, say, and believe.

66

WAKE UP

Once more Jesus addressed the crowd. He said,
"I am the Light of the world. He who follows
Me will not walk in the darkness, but will
have the Light of life" (John 8:12 AMP).

WHEN YOU WAKE UP TO THE FACT THAT YOU WERE CREATED
to be a Kingdom citizen, lights will come on in your mind. You
will leave behind the things that used to keep you stressed and
discontented, and you will look for opportunities to bring the
Kingdom into the world around you. Paul put it this way:

> *Have nothing to do with the fruitless deeds of dark-*
> *ness, but rather expose them. It is shameful even*
> *to mention what the disobedient do in secret. But*
> *everything exposed by the light becomes visible—*
> *and everything that is illuminated becomes a light.*
> *This is why it is said: "Wake up, sleeper, rise from the*
> *dead, and Christ will shine on you." Be very care-*
> *ful, then, how you live—not as unwise but as wise,*

making the most of every opportunity, because the days are evil. Therefore do not be foolish, but understand what the Lord's will is (Ephesians 5:11-17 NIV).

We are from Heaven, and we live on the earth, having brought all of Heaven's authority with us.

When you wake up and reorient yourself as a reborn citizen of the Kingdom of Light, the King will shine on you and His light will expose every bit of darkness in you. He will expose your bad decisions, your irresponsible behavior. He will show you where you have been keeping bad company and how you waste money. Not only will He show you what is wrong in your life, He will go on to show you what to do about it. He will help you gather up all the knowledge and understanding you have accumulated, and He'll show you how to apply it.

Knowledge and understanding are only comprehension—wisdom is the application of that information.

67

GOD'S VISION, YOUR DESTINY

"All this," David said, "I have in writing as a result of the Lord's hand on me, and he enabled me to understand all the details of the plan" (1 Chronicles 28:19 NIV).

GOD'S KINGDOM IS VERY PRACTICAL. EVERYTHING YOU HAVE learned up to now—the theories and principles, together with this great revelation you have about the Kingdom—applies to real-life situations. That is what Paul meant when he said, "making the most of every opportunity" in Ephesians 5:16. Time is limited and evil has had the upper hand for too long. By continuing to seek the Kingdom with passion, you may find that the King will redeem everything you lost through your mistakes.

You will understand more clearly what the King wants you to do. He will organize your schedule and dictate the company you are supposed to keep. His will includes every detail of your life. The will of God is always focused on the best for you—always.

At last you will understand why certain things had to happen. God will start to show you a vision for your life—your destiny in life. However, He will rarely let you see the steps of how to get there. This is because part of His plan is the process itself. He wants you to keep exercising your citizenship privileges and trusting in Him.

Joseph could never have viewed all of his seeming setbacks as steps to his destiny, but God knew what He was doing when He allowed him to be thrown in a pit—a pit that happened to be located along the route of the slave traders who would pull him out and take him to Egypt. Read Genesis chapters 37–50 to review the whole wonderful story. It is an excellent example of someone whose life belonged to God.

With awakened passion, make the most of every Kingdom opportunity.

68

A SECOND CHANCE

*The earth is the Lord's, and everything in it. The world
and all its people belong to him* (Psalm 24:1 NLT).

WHEN ADAM MISMANAGED HIS ASSIGNMENT, GOD TOOK IT
away from him. The same thing happens to us. Whatever we
mismanage, we lose. Whatever we manage with God's help,
we improve.

Managing the planet doesn't mean we become superheroes
or knights in shining armor who sweep away the opposition
and conquer the world. Our management takes place in our
own homes and neighborhoods, in our places of employment.
We manage our own bodies by eating the right foods and getting enough sleep. We manage our marriages by spending time
cultivating them. We manage our jobs and our salaries by getting to work on time and working diligently until quitting time.

Thanks to the King's guidance, our steps take us to the
right places at the right times. Once in a while, we know what
it is like to be given a bigger assignment.

Adam lost the real estate he had been given to manage. We have been given a second chance. Now that Jesus has come as the Second Adam, our authority has been restored. The kingship of God has an opportunity to prevail.

I hope you realize that God doesn't hand you gifts from His storehouse just because you call yourself a Christian or even because you are righteous. He gives you what you need for your management assignment. He will let you keep managing what He owns as long as you manage it well. If you handle your money and other possessions well, He will give you more to manage. That is Kingdom thinking, and the more we think that way, the better off we will be.

The Kingdom is here, now—manage it well.

69

WISDOM

*If any of you lacks wisdom [to guide him
through a decision or circumstance], he is to ask
of [our benevolent] God, who gives to everyone
generously and without rebuke or blame, and
it will be given to him* (James 1:5 AMP).

YOU CAN HAVE A PhD AND STILL BE STUPID. IT IS NOT
enough to learn information and understand it. You have to
know how to apply what you have learned if you want to gain
the highest level, which is wisdom.

Some people think they can be happy if they can only learn
enough truth. The Bible has this to say about such people, who
are "*always learning and never able to come to the knowledge of the
truth*" (2 Timothy 3:7 NKJV). Knowledge by itself, even when
the information is not false but true, is only the first step on the
way to wisdom.

Knowledge is important, however, because it does need to
come first. You need knowledge in order to get understanding

and comprehension. Finally, after you have grown in both knowledge and understanding, you are ready for wisdom.

Not only is wisdom the highest of the three, it leads us straight to the throne room of the Kingdom of God. Another verse in the Bible puts it this way: *"But of Him you are in Christ Jesus, who became for us wisdom from God"* (1 Corinthians 1:30 NKJV). Notice it doesn't say Jesus Christ, who became for us knowledge. Knowledge is only step number one. Jesus Christ became for us wisdom—because His presence leads us into the full application of all truth and righteousness, in which our knowledge can come into play.

"God has united you with Christ Jesus. For our benefit God made him to be wisdom itself. Christ made us right with God; he made us pure and holy, and he freed us from sin" (1 Corinthians 1:30 NLT).

70

KNOWLEDGE COMES FIRST

Give glory to the Lord your God before it is too late. Acknowledge him before he brings darkness upon you, causing you to stumble and fall on the darkening mountains. For then, when you look for light, you will find only terrible darkness and gloom (Jeremiah 13:16 NLT).

THE FUNDAMENTAL IMPORTANCE OF KNOWLEDGE CAN BE illustrated by a well-known story. Here is my version of it:

An elderly couple won first prize in a raffle: a free ten-day cruise. They had never been on a cruise before. In fact, they had never been anywhere, and they didn't know anything about traveling. They had lived in the same dirty little house for decades, and they had always pinched their pennies.

When they found out they had won, they were so embarrassed they didn't know what to do. So they packed a pitiful bundle of clothes, went down to the dock, and boarded the cruise ship. They showed their tickets, and the ticket-taker welcomed them aboard. The man and his wife wandered around the decks of the ship, just taking everything in. They had never seen so much beauty. They had never seen such well-dressed people. They had never seen so much activity. They had never used an elevator before.

They were shown to their cabin, which was on one of the highest decks, second from the top. When they got into their room, they touched their bed. They touched the floor. They ran their hands along the wall. They looked through the window and just stood there in amazement. It was like Heaven.

After they had settled in, they took out some crackers and cheese and packets of Kool-Aid. They mixed up a cool drink and just sat on the bed looking out the window as they ate. They were so excited to be on the ship.

Day after day it was the same. They would peep out their door at all of the well-dressed passengers running past, and they would close the door again and say, "Yippee! This is wonderful." They would look out the window and see the ocean and say, "Oh, this is just like Heaven. And they would enjoy some of their crackers and cheese and drink some of their Kool-Aid for breakfast, lunch, and dinner, three times a day.

Jesus said, "I came that they may have and enjoy life, and have it in abundance [to the full, till it overflows]" (John 10:10 AMP).

71

KNOWLEDGE COMES FIRST, CONTINUED

Give glory to the Lord your God before it is too late. Acknowledge him before he brings darkness upon you, causing you to stumble and fall on the darkening mountains. For then, when you look for light, you will find only terrible darkness and gloom (Jeremiah 13:16 NLT).

AFTER FIVE DAYS PASSED, THE CAPTAIN BECAME CONCERNED. What had happened to those two people?

On the ninth day, the captain became so uneasy about them that he sent one of his assistants to check on the couple. He knocked on the door. "Come in!" they said.

There they were, sitting on the floor on a sheet from the bed having a picnic on the floor. Wrappers from their crackers and cheese were all over the floor. They smiled up at him. "We are so thrilled to be on this ship. Thank you all, sir, for showing us your hospitality."

The assistant just stood in the doorway in shock. He didn't know what to say when he realized they had never left their room for nine days. Finally, he gulped and said, "Excuse me, madam and sir, were you in this room all along?

"Yes, we are so happy. Thank you so much for allowing us to have this room. It's been wonderful."

He said, "You never came out of the room to enjoy the entertainment, food, and all the rest?"

"Oh, no! We could not afford that."

Realizing something was wrong, the man asked to see their tickets. "Yes, sir," the woman said as she went to her purse, took out her ticket, and handed it to him.

He looked at the ticket, then looked up and said, "Didn't you read your ticket? Didn't you realize that your ticket gave you access to everything on the ship: all the food you can eat, all the games, all the swimming pools, all the spas, all the saunas? You could have had everything for free!"

But by the time they finished talking, the ship had returned to the dock. It was too late. They didn't know in time.

Jesus said, "I came that they may have and enjoy life, and have it in abundance [to the full, till it overflows]" (John 10:10 AMP).

72

DESTROYED FOR LACK OF KNOWLEDGE

My people are destroyed for lack of knowledge [of My law, where I reveal My will] (Hosea 4:6 AMP).

TOO MANY PEOPLE GO THEIR WHOLE LIVES WITHOUT UNDER-standing their country—Heaven—even when everything we need to know is given to us in the Bible, God's Word.

When I first heard the story of the elderly couple, it reminded me of God's cry for humanity in the book of Hosea: *"My people are destroyed for lack of knowledge"* (Hosea 4:6 KJV). I thought of the Kingdom of God, because it is the same with most of us, where the Kingdom is concerned. We don't know much of anything about it, even those of us who know we have got a free ticket. So we sell ourselves far short of all that the Kingdom offers. We skip right over the words of the Bible that explain the many ways the Kingdom works. We are as igno-rant as new babies about the citizenship we have just been born into.

As newborn human babies, we certainly didn't know anything at all about our citizenship. I was born in Bain Town in the Bahamas, but I didn't know a thing about the Bahamas for a long time. I was a baby. After a while, I began to learn things. As time went on, I began to understand what it meant to be a citizen of the Bahamas. It took a longer time to understand my citizenship in the Kingdom of Heaven.

How many people go their whole lives without understanding their country? They could enjoy full citizenship, but they know nothing about how it works, what rights and privileges it brings, nothing about the laws. They stay ignorant all their lives and live on the equivalent of cheese and crackers.

My desire is for everybody to throw their cheese and crackers overboard and walk to the buffet so you can enjoy the journey as much as the destination. The whole Kingdom is at your disposal; did you know?

God's Word is filled to overflowing with promises of an abundant life. Enjoy!

73

JESUS, THE APPLICATION OF KNOWLEDGE

*Until John the Baptist, the law of Moses and the
messages of the prophets were your guides. But now
the Good News of the Kingdom of God is preached,
and everyone is eager to get in* (Luke 16:16 NLT).

ALL THE KNOWLEDGE CONTAINED IN THE PAGES OF THE OLD
Testament could not fulfill God's promises of restoration of
the Kingdom—until Jesus came. As soon as He drew His
first human breath, that knowledge—much of which was
prophetic foreknowledge—began to grow into full wisdom.
Jesus explained: *"Do not think that I came to destroy the Law or
the Prophets. I did not come to destroy but to fulfill"* (Matthew
5:17 NKJV).

The Law and the Prophets were not superseded when the
King arrived on the planet; they were fulfilled in Him. They
represented the knowledge about the Kingdom, and Jesus
brought the application of that knowledge.

If you skim the various books of the Old Testament, you will understand what I am saying here. Start with the "big five" books, which are known as the Pentateuch (meaning "five books"): Genesis, Exodus, Leviticus, Numbers, Deuteronomy. In these books, the ceremonial laws that God gave to Moses are laid out in great detail.

Next we come to the book of Joshua, which describes the people of Israel after they had come into the Promised Land. Joshua's job was to settle the people and teach them the ways of God's Kingdom. As we proceed through the books of the Old Testament, the Kingdom story unfolds.

Jesus's presence on earth fulfilled all the promises and prophecies declared in the Old Testament so we can live free today.

74

PREPARING THE WAY

*"Behold, I send My messenger, and he will prepare
the way before Me. And the Lord, whom you seek,
will suddenly come to His temple, even the Messenger
of the covenant, in whom you delight. Behold, He is
coming," says the Lord of hosts* (Malachi 3:1 NKJV).

EVERY PROPHET, EVERY JUDGE, AND EVERY KING IN THE
Scriptures had something to do with preparing the way for the
coming of King Jesus. The judges and kings (the Law) embod-
ied justice and the divinely human rights of the Kingdom. The
prophets glimpsed the future and pronounced that a Messiah
would come. Together, they represent the Law and the Prophets. Who were some of these people?

After the book of Joshua, the book of Judges gives us
vignettes about the judges of Israel, men and women like Deb-
orah, who took over an army and routed the invading enemy to
protect the people who were being attacked. All of the judges
of Israel exercised their power to ascertain and establish the

rights of the citizens of Israel. The short book of Ruth appears next because it describes the lineage of the Messiah, naming His earthly ancestors. First and Second Kings introduce us to one of the greatest prophets of all time, Elijah, and his disciple Elisha. Both of them demonstrated the extreme power of the Kingdom of God more than the other prophets did. In fact, Elijah came to represent the very term "prophet" better than anybody else, just as Moses represented the term "law."

First and Second Samuel give us a look at the time when the people of Israel started asking for their first king. God wanted them to wait because He would be their King, but they would not wait. They wanted to have an earthly king like the other nations did. The prophet Samuel anointed Saul to be king, but Saul did not carry the crown with honor. Next came King David, who pleased God and ruled for a long time, giving us many illustrations of the Kingdom of God. The psalms that David wrote are all about Kingdom living. (Psalms are songs that show us how glorious God the King is. The book of Psalms is about a King, written by a king.) Besides establishing a kingdom that would become the model for understanding the Kingdom of Heaven, David himself was part of the lineage of the Messiah.

*Only Jesus, the Son of God, was and is the
Savior of the colony of earth—the One who left
the Kingdom of Heaven to save a dying world.*

75

LINES OF CONNECTION

He [Jesus] *said to them, "How foolish you are, and how slow to believe all that the prophets have spoken! Did not the Messiah have to suffer these things and then enter his glory?"* (Luke 24:25-26 NIV)

AFTER JESUS CAME TO THE EARTH COLONY, HE LIVED AND worked for thirty-three years; He suffered the crucifixion and rose from the grave. One day He was walking down a road with some of His old friends. At first they did not recognize Him, because, of course, they thought He was dead. As they walked, Jesus went through the Scriptures with them, explaining, probably in-depth, how all of the early Scriptures pointed to Him, the coming Messiah. When He finished, their eyes were opened and they realized He was the One, the Messiah, who was talking with them. (See Luke 24:13-34.) Jesus had established lines of connection well before that time.

I have always been highly interested in something that happened on what we now call the Mount of Transfiguration.

(The same story is told in three of the Gospels: Matthew 17, Mark 9, and Luke 9.) Jesus took three of His disciples up on a mountain. While they were with Him, who should appear out of the air but Moses and Elijah, who had been long dead.

Why those two? Because they represent the Law and the Prophets the most completely. Jesus did not take His disciples up on that mountain in order to show off His power. He went to have a meeting to pick up the baton. He went to close two books so He could open another. As He said in Luke 16:16, the Law and the Prophets were preached from the time of Moses to the time of Jesus's forerunner John the Baptist. Those are the only two things that could have been preached during that time. But all pointed toward the Kingdom, which arrived on the scene with the Son of God, Jesus.

We must never cut the lines of communication that the King has established between us through Jesus His Son and the Holy Spirit our Comforter.

76

BIBLICAL KNOWLEDGE

Jesus said, "You search the Scriptures because you think they give you eternal life. But the Scriptures point to me!" (John 5:39 NLT)

WHEN FIRST STEPPING INTO GOD'S KINGDOM, THE FIRST kind of knowledge we need is the knowledge of our constitutional rights in this new country. And because the Bible is the Constitution of the Kingdom of God, that is where we need to go to find out our constitutional rights. The Bible is like a contract or a covenant between the King and His citizens, and it tells us how to maintain our legal status. Of course we cannot follow its guidelines if we do not know what it says.

This can be a problem in any country. Have you ever read the constitution of your own country? The average person never does. We have no idea what is rightfully ours, so we can't even argue for our rights from a legal standpoint. We do not even know when we have been deprived of something that belongs to us by law. (Have you noticed that most politicians are lawyers? They know something that the rest of us do not know, and they can use it to their advantage.)

The person who knows the law cannot be manipulated—and this applies to the Kingdom of God just as much as it does to other countries. The greatest example of this occurred when the devil tested Jesus in the wilderness. How did Jesus win? He quoted Scripture. (See Matthew 4:1-11, Mark 1:12-13, Luke 4:113.) Jesus did not resort to rebuking the devil or binding him or casting him out. Jesus just spoke a few words from the book of Deuteronomy and whipped the tempter.

We must immerse ourselves in God's
Word to overcome every trick of the devil.

77

DEPENDENCY, THE KEY TO PROSPERITY

We have heard of your faith in Christ Jesus [how you lean on Him with absolute confidence in His power, wisdom, and goodness], and of the [unselfish] love which you have for all the saints (God's people) (Colossians 1:4 AMP).

JESUS KNEW WHAT TO SAY TO THE TEMPTER BECAUSE HE HAD immersed Himself in the written Word of God, and the Holy Spirit brought the right words to His mind when He needed them—just as the Spirit can do with us if we too read the Bible seeking understanding. Reading the Bible gives you legal power. Dependency on the Scriptures is the key to our prosperity.

Knowing what the Bible says will keep you from taking matters into your own hands. It will help you to trust the King to take care of you. Most have been raised in a society that teaches us to depend on nobody but ourselves. We learn how to protect ourselves and how to hang on to what we own. We find it hard to submit to anybody, and we don't want anybody else controlling our lives. But, when we come into the Kingdom of God, we must change our minds and hearts or Jesus can't really help us very much. Yes, we pray and ask Him for help—but then we oftentimes go ahead of Him and help ourselves. Our contingency plans are proof of the power of the spirit of independence. We pray and then we answer our own prayers—that is our old culture.

When I say that, I am not advocating the "prosperity doctrine" that some people preach. You can't just "name it and claim it" because you happen to want something nice. There is no such thing in the Bible as a prosperity doctrine. Jesus never preached on prosperity. He never had to, because in the Kingdom, it is irrelevant.

In the Kingdom, prosperity is a byproduct. When we seek first the Kingdom, all the things we need in order to prosper and flourish will be supplied for us. Getting into the Kingdom comes first, which places you in a position of complete dependence.

Lean on King Jesus and you will be
supplied with all you need—guaranteed.

78

BACK ON TRACK

*This hope is a strong and trustworthy anchor for
our souls. It leads us through the curtain into God's
inner sanctuary. Jesus has already gone in there for
us. He has become our eternal High Priest in the
order of Melchizedek* (Hebrews 6:19-20 NLT).

JESUS CAME TO EARTH TO SET THE PEOPLE OF THE EARTH
back on course by bringing in His Kingdom, to fulfill all of the
predictions and the foreshadows that had come since the time
of Adam. The prophets had spoken about a coming King. All
of the earlier earthly judges and kings had portrayed Him to
some extent. Suddenly He was here, and He won back men
and women everywhere, inviting them to become His breth-
ren, citizens of the Kingdom in the fullest sense.

Far from being as limited in scope and power as a new religion, His mission was to restore Heaven to earth. He came to
render the application of the Law and the Prophets, to bring
divine wisdom where only knowledge and understanding had

been before. The following is a list of what Jesus's coming means for us. Jesus came to:

- *Restore the government of God.* "For unto us...a Son is given; and the government will be upon his shoulder. ...Of the increase of his government and peace there will be no end, upon the throne of David and over his kingdom, to order it and establish it with judgment and justice" (Isaiah 9:6-7 KJV).

- *Restore Kingdom laws on earth.* Every country is built on laws. The Kingdom is built on God's Law as given to Moses.

- *Restore the values of Heaven.* Every colony reflects the values and culture of its parent government, and the Kingdom of God is no exception.

- *Restore citizenship of Heaven.* Once you get citizenship, you get all the others, and once you get all the others, you have citizenship.

So when Jesus said to the people, "Repent, for the Kingdom of God has arrived" (see Matthew 4:17), He was saying, "Change your thinking, because another country has returned to earth. It used to be here when Adam was alive, but Adam got rid of it. The prophets have been telling you that I would be coming, and now I have come. I came to bring the Kingdom of Heaven back to earth."

Jesus, the Son of God, brought the Kingdom of Heaven to earth so we can live like co-heirs with Him.

79

No Contingency Plans

Jesus said to him, "Get up and go [on your way].
Your faith [your personal trust in Me and
your confidence in God's power] has restored
you to health" (Luke 17:19 AMP).

In INDEPENDENT-MINDED CULTURES, MIRACLES DO NOT
happen as often, because people have their own contingency
plans in their back pockets in case prayer doesn't work. When
your trust level is low, your Kingdom life will be almost zero.

This bothers people, especially Americans, who see dependence on God as a cop-out. (That's the American term for it.
Others would say it's a weak jelly-back way to live.) They don't
appreciate the value of dependency. They don't understand
that the lower you go before a king, the higher he lifts you.
God is the King of the universe. He owns it. The more you
humble yourself before the Owner, the more you can expect
to be exalted. Jesus said, *"For those who exalt themselves will be*

humbled, and those who humble themselves will be exalted" (Matthew 23:12 NIV).

You know why more miracles happen in countries where the spirit of independence is not strong? Because in those countries, people do not have an alternative "Excedrin" to take. When you get a headache in a remote village in Africa, you need God.

Less self-reliance and more God-reliance leads to an intimate relationship with your Creator.

80

PERSISTENCE PAYS OFF

A widow of that city came to him repeatedly, saying,
"Give me justice in this dispute with my enemy." The
judge ignored her for a while, but finally he said to
himself, "I don't fear God or care about people, but
this woman is driving me crazy. I'm going to see
that she gets justice, because she is wearing me out
with her constant requests!" (Luke 18:3-5 NLT)

I LEARNED THE POWERFUL VALUE OF KNOWING MY RIGHTS AS A citizen when I first began my ministry in 1980. Within a few years, we wanted to start a radio broadcast. When we went to the station to inquire, they said, "Okay, no problem. If you can pay for it, you can have your program—during the 'graveyard shift' between midnight and six in the morning." They told us that was the only time of day when they played religious programs.

I told them we wanted a program that would be aired during drive-time in the late afternoon, about five o'clock. They said that was impossible in this country. It didn't matter that we had the money to buy the hour and that we were legitimate citizens.

I did not give up. I went up the corporate ladder and even the guys at the top said, "No, we can't do that." I went higher. I made an appointment with the government minister who was over broadcasting in the Bahamas.

I said, "Sir, this is what we want to do and the corporation says we cannot." I showed him our plan. He said no. He said it was impossible because it was not Bahamian custom to have religious broadcasting on during the daylight hours.

So I had to get tough. I said, "Look, I am a citizen. I have a product. I have the money. I can buy the time, and it is my right to do so. As a matter of fact, I would not mind taking the government to court…." That got his attention. I continued, "If I take the government to court, I will win because the constitution says…" and I started quoting the constitution of the Bahamas.

Nobody had ever been that determined. He promised to bring it up at the next meeting of parliament, and he did. After three weeks, they called me in. "We have never done this before, but we are going to let you do it." We became the first group in the history of the Bahamas to play inspirational Christian music on the radio. Our program aired every Thursday afternoon between 5 and 6 p.m. It was called "Music to Believe In."

Never give up when the Lord gives you
a vision, a plan to bring Him glory.

81

♕

KINGDOM
RESPONSIBILITIES

*If you [really] love Me, you will keep and obey
My commandments* (John 14:15 AMP).

YOU ARE A CITIZEN OF A COUNTRY ON EARTH, AND I HOPE you are a citizen of the Kingdom of Heaven. Remember that your citizenship does not mean only that the government is responsible for taking care of you, but that you have a responsibility to the government as well. It is a two-way street, and the traffic goes both ways. Just as it is for you as a citizen of your earthly country, so also in the Kingdom of God are you held accountable to the government by means of its constitution—in this case, the Bible. You can be a much happier and more productive citizen when you understand your responsibilities.

Sad to say, many people do not want to shoulder their responsibilities. They are glad God has saved them, but they don't necessarily want to obey Him. They don't understand that their obedience is a way of expressing their appreciation.

Jesus Christ Himself put it concisely: *"If you love Me, keep My commandments"* (John 14:15 NKJV).

They also fail to acknowledge that the rights that they enjoy as citizens, while they can't be *earned* because they have been given as privileges, they must be *maintained* through simple obedience to the laws of the land.

Remember that your citizenship does not mean only that the government is responsible for taking care of you, but that you have a responsibility to the government as well.

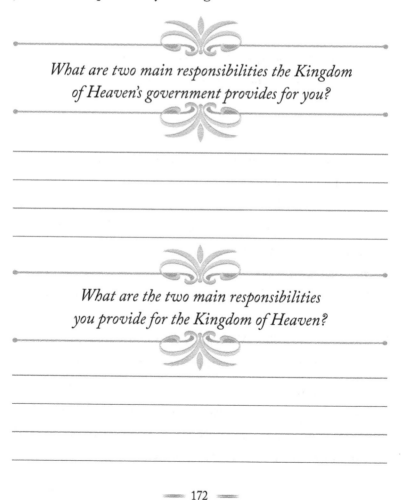

What are two main responsibilities the Kingdom of Heaven's government provides for you?

What are the two main responsibilities you provide for the Kingdom of Heaven?

82

AUTHORITY IS GOOD

Authorities do not strike fear in people who are doing right, but in those who are doing wrong. Would you like to live without fear of the authorities? Do what is right, and they will honor you (Romans 13:3 NLT).

AUTHORITY IS A GOOD THING, AND YOU NEVER OUTGROW your need for it. Can you imagine a plant saying this to the soil? "That is enough. You have been holding me down for all these years. I'm out of here, and I'm taking my root with me." What would happen if a plant did that? It would die, sooner or later. The absence of authority brings self-destruction.

Fish were created to submit to water. If a fish decides to move out from under its authority, you do not need to punish it, because it will die. The safest place for the fish to be is *submitted*. Surely you have seen a fish out of water. It gasps and flips and flops, trying as hard as it can to get back into water. I know people like that. They try this and that and wonder why nothing is working. When young people leave home too early, life can be very tough for a long time. It is the same principle. It is time to get back under authority.

Part of submission to authority is patience. The authorities over us keep us from crashing into each other—if we obey their directives. Freedom has boundaries, always. In the Kingdom, if the King says, "You are free to eat from any other tree, but do not eat from this tree," He has good reasons. Disobedience is not the best way to find out about the repercussions.

Do what is right and live without fear.

83

AUTHORITY'S POWER

The centurion answered and said, "Lord... only speak
a word, and my servant will be healed. For I also am
a man under authority, having soldiers under me.
And I say to this one, 'Go,' and he goes; and to another,
'Come,' and he comes; and to my servant, 'Do this,'
and he does it." When Jesus heard it, He marveled, and
said... "I have not found such great faith, not even
in Israel! ... Go your way; and as you have believed,
so let it be done for you." And his servant was healed
that same hour (Matthew 8:8-10,13 NKJV).

WE LIKE TO BE AROUND POWERFUL PEOPLE, BUT WE NEED TO
ask ourselves, "Is this person's power under authority?" Power
combines ability and energy and force, while authority is the
right and permission to use that power. Authority is the right
to use power effectively, not because you could, but because you
should. Authority makes power legal.

Therefore, authority is more important than power. Teen-
agers may have the power to leave home, but they do not yet

have the authority to leave. A person may be very aggressive and loud in speaking, but if they do not have authority, their words will not carry weight.

Submission to authority is what makes a person effective.

See also how the centurion's military experience gave him a more complete understanding of the way authority works. He was completely submitted to the Roman emperor and any other commanders who ranked above him. He had at least a hundred soldiers who reported directly to him. (The title *centurion* is related to the word *century*, which indicates one hundred.) Probably he had been watching Jesus. He may have seen Him healing the sick, raising the dead, casting out demons, and more. Obviously, this man Jesus had power. Obviously some higher Authority was guiding Him. He knew that a person's performance depended upon his obedience to the instructions he had been given.

In the same way, if we want to experience God's best for our lives, we must stay under His authority—then we will be heard and answered.

When you submit to God's authority,
you will live your best life.

84

RIGHTEOUSNESS

*Righteousness [moral and spiritual
integrity and virtuous character] exalts a
nation...* (Proverbs 14:34 AMP).

JESUS WANTS US TO SEEK FIRST HIS KINGDOM AND, ALONG
with it, His righteousness (see Matthew 6:33). "Righteousness" is the same as submission to His authority within the
Kingdom of God. By becoming righteous, you uphold the
authority of the Kingdom—which in turn upholds you. This
is nothing like other religions, where "submitting" involves
trying to keep your god happy. You are not bringing gifts to an
altar or lighting incense and chanting in front of a statue. You
are not contributing money or going through all sorts of rituals
to obligate your king to look after you. You are not appeasing
the authorities.

When you submit to God's authority, He shows you what
is next. He helps change your behavior to one that benefits you
daily. He even helps you seek more of His righteousness. By

remaining close to Him, you guarantee that the authority of the government of the Kingdom will be extended—through you—wherever you go.

When you keep the law, you secure your God-given authority over the kingdom of darkness.

The laws to which you are submitting are heavenly laws, such as, *"Love your enemies, do good to those who hate you, bless those who curse you, and pray for those who spitefully use you"* (Luke 6:27-28 NKJV). So as you use Kingdom love—which is powerful enough to extinguish all powers of darkness— you keep yourself under the protection of God while fulfilling your assignment.

"The righteous will be happy to see the wicked destroyed, and the innocent will laugh in contempt" (Job 22:19 NLT).

85

GOD IS LOVE

Whoever does not love does not know God,
because God is love (1 John 4:8 NIV).

HATRED WILL SHUT DOWN YOUR FAITH, AND SO WILL BLIND religious rituals. So submitting to the God of love even more completely is to your own benefit as much as the benefit of those around you.

You do not get things from God just because you ask. You get things from the government of Heaven because you keep the laws of the country. It is not enough to talk about the laws in church on Sunday or at Bible study on Wednesday—you need to read the Law Book as often as possible and follow those laws faithfully. The minute you stop doing that, you start removing yourself from the King's protection and help.

A lot of people think they can get away with sin just because nobody's looking. That is audacious, to say the least. We come to God and say, "God, heal me (but I'm still going to take drugs)." Or we say, "I'm going to sleep with that woman

I am not married to, but I want You to bless my business and pay my bills." We demand things while we are in disobedience.

Instead of breaking laws and hoping you can get away with it, why not start obeying laws that you would not mind getting caught obeying? For example, see if you can get caught loving your brother. See if somebody can catch you paying your tithe. Let somebody catch you forgiving someone who hurt you, or spot you committing an act of kindness. Gossip about somebody who has lived with his wife for forty-two years without strife; that would be a wonderful thing to gossip about. The laws of this Kingdom country are wonderful, every one of them.

Do right intentionally all the time,
and the King is going to bless you.

86

KEYS TO THE KINGDOM AND VICTORY

*[Jesus said,] "I will give you the keys (authority) of
the kingdom of heaven; and whatever you bind [forbid,
declare to be improper and unlawful] on earth will have
[already] been bound in heaven, and whatever you loose
[permit, declare lawful] on earth will have [already]
been loosed in heaven"* (Matthew 16:19 AMP).

CITIZENS OF THE KINGDOM HAVE A RESPONSIBILITY TO learn the words of the Bible. We need to read it often, because we tend to forget what it says. We need to read it more often than we read the newspaper. When the devil attacked Jesus in the wilderness, His responses came straight from Scripture. He said, "It is written" (see Luke 4:1-13). Those words were His keys to the Kingdom and victory.

Jesus said, *"Most assuredly, I say to you, the Son can do nothing of Himself, but what He sees the Father do; for whatever He does, the Son also does in like manner"* (John 5:19 NKJV). He exercised the keys of Kingdom authority better than anyone before or since. Yet He, true Prince that He is, wants nothing more than for the citizens of His Kingdom to exercise those same keys.

You need to do only two things: 1) seek the Kingdom in order to get into citizenship; and 2) seek the King's righteousness in order to stay in it. In other words, stay aligned with the King. When you stay aligned with the King and His government, you obligate Him to take care of you. All of the promises in the Constitution remain accessible to you, as needed. Things that you would otherwise need to fight for will come your way with no sweat.

"It is written" is the key to the Kingdom of Heaven and to your everyday victory—read God's Word faithfully.

87

PRAYER

[Jesus said,] *"In this manner, therefore, pray: Our Father in heaven, hallowed be Your name. Your kingdom come. Your will be done on earth as it is in heaven. Give us this day our daily bread. And forgive us our debts, as we forgive our debtors. And do not lead us into temptation, but deliver us from the evil one. For Yours is the kingdom and the power and the glory forever. Amen"* (Matthew 6:9-13 NKJV).

PRAYER ITSELF DOES NOT GET THINGS DONE—POSITIONING in prayer gets things done. The best preparation for prayer is your obedience to the laws of God. Many times, the reason God can't help you is because you ask Him last. Only by staying aligned with the Lawgiver and Judge, through the work of the Spirit and Son, can you prevail.

Have you noticed that if you have just sinned, you are unable to find boldness in prayer? When you break God's law, it shuts down your prayer life. You have canceled your right to appeal. *"If I regard iniquity in my heart, the Lord will not hear me"* (Psalm 66:18 KJV). The prophet Isaiah stated it clearly: *"But your iniquities have separated you from your God; and your sins have hidden His face from you, so that He will not hear"* (Isaiah 59:2 NKJV).

It won't matter how loudly you beg for mercy and cry out for help, because God does not bless you because you cry; He blesses you because you qualify. Believers have authority in prayer as long as they have maintained their side of their covenant with the King, a legal agreement. You don't have to go before Him with theatrics or hysterics any more than a lawyer would go before an earthly judge that way. You just have to be a citizen in good standing, and the Judge will hear your case.

"The earnest prayer of a righteous person has great power and produces wonderful results" (James 5:16 NLT).

88

BEING RELIGIOUS
IS NOT ENOUGH

*So now we can rejoice in our wonderful new
relationship with God because our Lord Jesus Christ
has made us friends of God* (Romans 5:11 NLT).

THE GOAL OF GOD WAS NEVER RELIGION, BUT RATHER SOME-
thing I call "rulership through relationship." I have described
His original plan to have Adam and all the people who followed him rule over and manage the planet, and the close
association between the words *dominate* and *kingdom,* which
you might call rulership. But rulership alone was never God's
goal, because it must be based on a relationship with Him.

We come into the Kingdom of God exclusively through
establishing a personal relationship with the King and His Son
Jesus. The Son opened the way to this relationship when He
became a man Himself. His Spirit lives inside us, and we begin
a lifelong process of growing more and more into His likeness.
The apostle named Paul summed it up best when he wrote:

> *Therefore, if anyone is in Christ, he is a new creation; old things have passed away; behold, all things have become new. Now all things are of God, who has reconciled us to Himself through Jesus Christ, and has given us the ministry of reconciliation.... Now then, we are ambassadors for Christ, as though God were pleading through us: we implore you on Christ's behalf, be reconciled to God* (2 Corinthians 5:17-20 NKJV).

Those of us who have found the Kingdom know what it is—the Kingdom is the King. The more we learn about Him, the better it gets. We want to communicate to all of the other searchers what He is like. We have also been given the task to spread the Kingdom worldwide. We have been commissioned to show the world what the Kingdom of Heaven looks like. We have become diplomats for the department of Heaven that has colonized earth. In short, we are ambassadors for Christ Jesus.

Are you prepared, willing, and able to take on the task of spreading the Good News of the Kingdom of God and Heaven?

89

KINGDOM LIFESTYLE

And the Lord has greatly blessed my master; he has become a wealthy man. The Lord has given him flocks of sheep and goats, herds of cattle, a fortune in silver and gold (Genesis 24:35 NLT).

I WENT WITH A FEW OTHERS TO HAITI. THE BAHAMIAN ambassador picked us up at the airport, and we drove through the streets in a beautiful SUV. All around us was rubble. People were sleeping on the streets in the muck, yet we drove through all of that in air-conditioned comfort, sipping on cool drinks. The Bahamian flag was fluttering from the front of the SUV. I'm sure that the people we passed were wondering what country that flag represented, thinking to themselves, Wherever that flag comes from, I want to go there.

We arrived at the ambassador's large house in the hills, untouched by the recent earthquake. We walked into the house and were served a big breakfast of bacon, cheese, and grits, right there in the middle of all that poverty.

The ambassador took me to my bedroom that was as big as a house. He said, "You can sleep here tonight." I asked if he meant me and the brother who was with me. "Oh no, he has his own room. This is all for you." And he opened a curtain revealing a swimming pool full of blue water.

"Don't you feel guilty sometimes, your Excellency?" I asked.

"No. When you step into my car and drive through my gate, you enter the Bahamas." The property of an embassy is the same as the country it represents. It will always be as rich as the home country—never as poor as the country in which the embassy and the ambassador's house are situated.

The ambassador never had to fly to the Bahamas for his bacon and eggs or to enjoy a nice, air-conditioned house with a pool. He was experiencing the Bahamian lifestyle in another country.

Your assignment may seem insignificant to you, but the way you complete it is very important.

The Kingdom lifestyle—clean living, love-filled, and truly joyful—is ours wherever we may be stationed on the globe. This is a culture of plenty, and it makes people want to come to God.

Does your lifestyle, attitude, and perspective
reflect your Kingdom of Heaven ambassadorship?

90

YOU ARE A KINGDOM AMBASSADOR

*The master was full of praise. "Well done,
my good and faithful servant. You have been
faithful in handling this small amount, so now
I will give you many more responsibilities. Let's
celebrate together!"* (Matthew 25:21 NLT)

EVERY CITIZEN OF THE KINGDOM IS AN AMBASSADOR. AS YOU go to work tomorrow morning or stop to buy something that you need, remember that you are a citizen of Heaven *and* an ambassador for the Kingdom of Heaven. This is an important mindset, because you will not be much of an ambassador for the King if you forget your identity. He has conferred His authority on you, and He has given you an assignment—to represent Him wherever you go and spread the truth about the Kingdom you represent. Will you do that?

I pray that you will connect with your King on a daily basis, and that you will hear what He is saying to you. Your assignment may seem insignificant to you, but the way you complete it is vital. May your citizenship in the Kingdom equip you to be a true ambassador, and may the King commend you for your service: *"Well done, good and faithful servant! You have been faithful with a few things; I will put you in charge of many things. Come and share your master's happiness!"* (Matthew 25:21 NIV)—those are the words I hope you hear when you reach your home country, Heaven.

Choose to connect daily with the King
and listen for His voice in your life.

About Myles Munroe

(1954-2014)

Dr. Myles Munroe was more than a pastor, teacher, and author, he was a Christian statesman who became a catalytic thought leader for a whole generation of church leaders and Christ-followers. Dr. Munroe served as a pioneer and prophetic voice, summoning the church to embrace its heavenly inheritance now instead of just holding out for the afterlife.

From the truth-saturated pages of his Kingdom book series to his intense international speaking schedule, Dr. Munroe called the global church upward to embrace the holistic message of the Kingdom and discover the culture of Heaven, seeing as much as possible of that Kingdom culture enter into and transform present conditions.

Dr. Munroe's Kingdom message is crucial for the church today. In an era of great turmoil, uncertainty, and upheaval, Christians need to fully step into their Kingdom purpose. It is not time for Christianity to be intimidated by the encroaching darkness and retreat into hiding. It's time to reveal God's will and purpose on earth as in Heaven. This devotional is a compilation of one of Dr. Munroe's best-selling books, *Principle and Power of Kingdom Citizenship*.

Dr. Munroe's legacy lives on through Munroe Global, Inc., where his son, Myles Munroe, Jr., is the CEO/President, and through the Myles and Ruth Munroe Foundation, where their daughter, Charisa, is President. The goal of the ministries is to use the leadership lessons of the late great visionary Dr. Myles Munroe to create new opportunities for people to discover and put into action their life purpose. Also dedicated to the development of nations, one individual at a time, sharing Dr. Munroe's vision to reach the world with priceless principles of leadership and empowerment, spreading the Kingdom leadership message to the world.

From

Dr. Myles Munroe

Discover How to Live as a Citizen of God's Unshakable Kingdom

Are you ready to experience life on a new, supernatural level? Then it's time to take your place as a royal citizen in God's unshakable Kingdom.

For too long, *too many* followers of Christ have lived *beneath* their Kingdom inheritance. They are saved and set up for eternity in Heaven, yet they continue to live defeated and unfulfilling lives on Earth.

In this paradigm-shifting work by Dr. Myles Munroe, he presents the biblical blueprint for what it looks like for you to live as an empowered Kingdom citizen.

The Kingdom is not about going to Heaven one day after you die...it is about walking in the purpose and power of Heaven *today* while you are still living on Earth!

Purchase your copy wherever books are sold

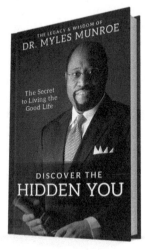

In the Right Hands, This Book Will Change Lives!

Most of the people who need this message will not be looking for this book. To change their lives, you need to **put a copy of this book in their hands.**

Our ministry is constantly seeking methods to find the people who need this anointed message to change their lives. **Will you help us reach these people?**

Extend this ministry by sowing three, five, ten, or *even more* books today and change people's lives for the better! Your generosity will be part of catalyzing the Great Awakening that many have been prophesying and praying for.

YOUR Prophetic COMMUNITY

Are you passionate about hearing God's voice, walking with Jesus, and experiencing the power of the Holy Spirit?

Destiny Image is a community of believers with a passion for equipping and encouraging you to live the prophetic, supernatural life you were created for!

We offer a fresh helping of practical articles, dynamic podcasts, and powerful videos from respected, Spirit-empowered, Christian leaders to fuel the holy fire within you.

Sign up now to get awesome content delivered to your inbox
destinyimage.com/sign-up

 Destiny Image